# HOCKEY TOUGH

## SAUL L. MILLER

Human Kinetics

## Library of Congress Cataloging-in-Publication Data

Miller, Saul, L.
    Hockey tough / Saul L. Miller.– Rev. ed.
        p. cm.
    Rev. ed. of: Complete player : Stoddart, 2001.
        ISBN 0-7360-5123-6 (soft cover)
    1. Hockey–Psychological aspects. 2. Hockey–Training. I. Miller,
Saul L. Complete player. II. Title.
        GV847.3.M55 2003
        796.96'0'19–dc21

                                                            2003007294
ISBN: 0-7360-5123-6

This book is a revised edition of *The Complete Hockey Player: The Psychology of Winning Hockey,* published in 2001 by Stoddart Publishing.

**Developmental Editor:** Cynthia McEntire; **Assistant Editors:** John Wentworth, Alisha Jeddeloh, Scott Hawkins; **Copyeditor:** Barbara Field; **Proofreader:** Kathy Bennett; **Indexer:** Susan Danzi Hernandez; **Graphic Designer:** Nancy Rasmus; **Graphic Artist:** Francine Hamerski; **Art and Photo Manager:** Dan Wendt; **Illustrators:** Dan Wendt, Roberto Sabas; **Cover Designer:** Jack W. Davis; **Photographer (cover):** Scott Cunningham/Getty Images; **Printer:** United Graphics

Human Kinetics books are available at special discounts for bulk purchase. Special editions or book excerpts can also be created to specification. For details, contact the Special Sales Manager at Human Kinetics.

Printed in the United States of America   10 9 8 7 6 5 4 3 2 1

**Human Kinetics**

Web site: www.HumanKinetics.com

*United States:* Human Kinetics
P.O. Box 5076
Champaign, IL 61825-5076
800-747-4457
e-mail: humank@hkusa.com

*Canada:* Human Kinetics
475 Devonshire Road Unit 100
Windsor, ON N8Y 2L5
800-465-7301 (in Canada only)
e-mail: orders@hkcanada.com

*Europe:* Human Kinetics
107 Bradford Road
Stanningley
Leeds LS28 6AT, United Kingdom
+44 (0) 113 255 5665
e-mail: hk@hkeurope.com

*Australia:* Human Kinetics
57A Price Avenue
Lower Mitcham, South
Australia 5062
08 8277 1555
e-mail: liahka@senet.com.au

*New Zealand:* Human Kinetics
P.O. Box 105-231, Auckland Central
09-523-3462
e-mail: hkp@ihug.co.nz

*To the guys I first played hockey with on the ice and snow of Ponsard Park in Montreal, to the NHLers who inspired us, and to all the parents and coaches who nurture a love of the game and a passion to excel.*

# CONTENTS

# FOREWORD

*Hockey tough* is an expression that characterizes the sport. Hockey is a tough, exciting, creative, physical game—a high-speed, contact, skill sport that challenges a player physically and mentally. A complete player needs more than skating and stick skills. He needs to be mentally tough. He must play with focus, determination, intensity, passion, and pride. To be consistently successful, he must be able to summon the energy, courage, and will to compete game after game and to maintain focus and composure in the heat of a real physical battle.

To compete successfully, a hockey player requires strength, determination, and discipline and the understanding and flexibility to play a role in the team's game. Although this may be true of many sports, to my mind, no sport demands more mental toughness than professional hockey.

*Hockey Tough* is about strengthening your mental game for hockey—or for any sport. The book reaffirms my own belief that having a strong mental game has been a major factor in my success. Saul Miller has captured the mental requirements of an athlete perfectly. *Hockey Tough* is an important book for any player, young or old.

**Mark Messier**
*New York Rangers*

# ACKNOWLEDGMENTS

I wish to thank the following people who contributed to my experience of the game and to the writing of this book.

To Ted Miller, Cynthia McEntire, Angel Guerra, Jim Gifford, Laara Maxwell, and Garfield Lindsay Miller for editorial comments and helpful suggestions.

Thanks also to hockey coaches Scotty Bowman, Kevin Constantine, Marc Crawford, Terry Crisp, Gary Davidson, Mark Ferner, Glen Hanlon, Mark Holick, Peter Horachek, Mike Keenan, George Kingston, Mitch Korn, Rick Lanz, Kevin McCarthy, Jack McIlhargey, Troy Mick, Andy Moog, Mike Murphy, Harry Neale, Roger Neilson, Brent Peterson, David Poile, Pat Quinn, Todd Richards, Doug Risebrough, Larry Robinson, Stan Smyl, Barry Trotz, and Bob Tunstead.

Thanks to Roger Neilson, a dedicated hockey man, a successful and innovative coach, and a kind and caring fellow.

I thank scouts Bob Berry, Bart Brady, Craig Channell, John Chapman, Ron Delorme, Frank Fay, and Mike Penny. Thank you to media relations people Chris Brumwell, Alex Gilchrist, Greg Harvey, and Reid Mitchell.

Thanks to trainers and physicians Larry Ashley, Dusan Benicky, Mike Burnstein, Pete Demers, Dan Redmond, Peter Twist, and Dr. Karen Johnston.

Most especially, I want to thank the players, both those I've worked with over the years and those who were kind enough to assist me on this project: Dennis Arkhipov, Adrian Aucoin, Derek Bekar, Ken Berry, Donald Brashear, Pavel Bure, Eric Christensen, Dan Cloutier, Matt Cooke, Andy Delmore, Ron Delorme, Ty Domi, Mike Dunham, Martin Erat, Bryan Ericsson, Vern Fiddler, Wade Flaherty, Jim Fox, Marian Gaborik, Gary Galley, Brent Gilchrist, Scott Gomez, Anders Hakansson, Adam Hall, Dan Hamhius, Glen Hanlon, Mark Hardy, Bret Hedican, Darby Hendrickson, Bill Houlder, Jamie Hudscroft, Cale Hulse, Bob Janycek, Andreas Johannsen, Curtis Joseph, Ed Jovanovski, Paul Kariya, Steve Kariya, Trent Klatt, Victor Kozlov, Denny Lambert, Rick Lanz, Grant Ledyard, David Legwand, Mario Lemieux, Morris Lukowich, Dave Mackey, Frank Mahovolich,

Brad May, Rollie Melanson, Scott Mellanby, Mark Messier, Alfie Michauld, Alexander Mogilny, Josh Morrow, Bill Muckalt, Markus Naslund, Jim Nill, Mattias Ohlund, Bobby Orr, Dennis Pederson, Larry Playfair, Chris Pronger, Craig Redmond, Luc Robitaille, Cliff Ronning, Dave Scatchard, Corey Schwab, Jeff Sharples, Billy Smith, Doug Smith, Peter Smrek, Stan Smyl, Garth Snow, Brent Sopel, Steve Staios, Peter Stastny, Dave Taylor, Joe Thornton, Kimmo Timonen, Jordin Tootoo, Scott Upshall, John Vanbeisbrouck, Joe Vandermeer, Tomas Vokoun, Eli Vorliceck, Scott Walker, Nick Wawrykow, Kevin Weekes, Dave "Tiger" Williams, Clarke Wilm, Jason York, Steve Yzerman, plus the players of the Milwaukee Admirals and Syracuse Crunch of the AHL, the Kamloops Blazers and Tri-City Americans of the WHL, the Langley Hornets and Surrey Eagles of the BCHL, and the Kelowna Minor Hockey Association.

# INTRODUCTION

*What is hockey tough?* More than any sport I've experienced, hockey places extreme demands on the mental capacities of the athlete. To be hockey tough is to have the ability to overcome these challenges. I see five keys to becoming hockey tough.

1. Hockey tough means having the desire and drive to be the best player you can be and the dedication to work hard to develop the physical and mental skills to be your best.

2. Being hockey tough means being hockey smart. It's having a positive, productive on-ice focus. It's knowing your job and being alert and tuned into executing effectively.

3. Hockey tough means being in control of your emotions. It's knowing how to energize and power up as well as how to maintain composure. It's working hard; staying focused; and not being distracted by pressure, fear, anger, or negativity.

4. Hockey tough means being determined and committed to doing what's necessary to improve your game and playing the team game to the best of your ability.

5. Hockey tough means having the strength and resilience to weather the bumps, bruises, frustrations, fatigue, highs, and lows of a long season. All of these hockey tough qualities can be enhanced with training.

*Hockey Tough* is a guide to becoming a more focused, positive, and productive hockey player. The book will provide answers to the questions that haunt players: Why do some players score lots of goals while others who have seemingly equal skills rarely score at all? How is it that some players are able to stay focused while others are easily distracted by the pressure and violence of the game? What is the best way to prepare for a game? Is there something a player can say to himself to help him play better? How do players get out of slumps? How do players keep themselves sharp and shift-ready despite sitting on the bench for long periods? How do players get up for the game shift after shift, night after night, throughout a long hockey season? How can players use visualization and imagery to be more effective? Why do defensemen use visualization more than forwards? How can recovering from injury be turned into a positive experience? What methods can increase confidence and sense of pride? What can players do to become mentally tougher? *Hockey Tough* explores all these issues and provides sport psychology coaching to help you become a more complete player.

I was discussing the hockey tough concept with Andreas Johannsen, a skillful NHL veteran, a solid team player, and Swedish all-star. Andreas liked the term. He mentioned how the North American game epitomizes hockey toughness. "Over here, the game is more physical. The players are bigger, the ice surface is smaller, there are more games and more travel. It's tough." Andreas continued, "But it's more than that. Here there is a different attitude to the game. There is an intense pressure to compete and perform. In the Swedish league, you can get away with playing a mediocre game. That's not the case in the NHL. The competitiveness is intense. There's no job security. Every night, every shift, you're expected to give 100 percent. And you've got to be mentally tough to do that."

# GAINING A MENTAL EDGE

When I talk to hockey teams around North America, I often begin by asking the players how many of them believe that increasing physical strength will improve on-ice performance. Usually, they all raise their hands. Then I ask how many of them are in some kind of workout program to increase physical strength. Again, almost everyone raises a hand. Next, I ask how many of them believe that increasing mental strengths will improve on-ice performance. After some hesitation, several players raise their hands. However, when I ask how many of them are actively doing something to increase their mental strengths, few if any hands are raised.

Kevin McCarthy, a former NHL defenseman and captain, now an NHL coach, told me, "Mental preparation is one area not stressed enough. So much time is spent on conditioning, both on and off the ice. We do the same drills and variations again and again, and almost nothing is done to improve a player's mental game. Yet when we talk about breakdowns, rarely if ever is it because of the player's physical attributes. Almost always, it has to do with *mental* lapses. Players are not ready to play. They're not focused. They are not in the right positions or where they're supposed to be. Learning how to mentally prepare, learning to anticipate, learning to play the game in your head are important in getting an edge and reacting consistently well in the game. This is especially true in the playoffs."

Kevin continued, "Some players don't handle pressure well. One solution to improve consistency, especially in high-pressure situations, is to develop a routine, something that you can use before a game and on the bench between shifts. That helps you refocus and get ready to go again in the next game or on the next shift."

Kevin's right. In preparing athletes to play hockey, most coaches emphasize the physical and technical aspects of the game. Drills stress skating, conditioning, puck control, passing, and shooting. The mental training aspect of hockey has been relatively ignored.

*Hockey Tough* addresses the imbalance in training through a discussion of psychological skills and mental training techniques that have helped a wide range of elite hockey players strengthen their mental game and become more focused, more confident, mentally tougher, more in control, and better prepared to play winning hockey. *Hockey Tough* is not a book for the beginner. It is for competitive players who want to maximize their abilities and develop the mental strengths and skills that will elevate on-ice performance.

# THE THREE "RIGHTS"

Sport psychology can be a valuable coaching resource. Players who consult with me are usually seeking improvement in some aspect of their game—improved scoring, better defensive play, or in the case of goaltenders, improved ability to stop the puck. Sometimes they are playing well but feel anxious. Or they are squeezing the stick, playing too tight, and the more they try, the less effective they seem to be. Some players want to learn how to be more focused, prepare better, develop better mental discipline, or feel more confident. Others have been injured and are looking for something to help them return to form. Still others are struggling to adapt to a system or to get along with a coach. Finally, there are those who consult me because they are having trouble getting up for games or coping with a multitude of distractions on and off the ice.

As a sport psychologist, I have worked with hockey players for more than 20 years, at both the NHL and developmental levels. I've observed that at all levels, there are three basics to winning the mental game of hockey:

1. Right focus. Plain and simple, it's knowing what it is you want to do on the ice, staying tuned in, and working to make that happen.

2. Right feeling. By that I mean creating and maintaining feelings that help you to play your best. For some that means feeling energized and up; for others it's feeling more calm, confident, centered, and in control. Right feelings also mean not being distracted by fear, anger, and pressure.

3. Right attitude. A winning hockey attitude is characterized by the motivation, commitment, confidence, and love of the game needed to persevere and excel.

The examples presented in this book are all based on real players and real on-ice experiences. To maintain the confidentiality of clients past and present, I have changed the identities and names of some of the players and coaches described in the examples. The techniques described are applicable to all players regardless of gender. Since most of my clients have been male, for simplicity, I use a masculine pronoun when referring to players.

## USING *HOCKEY TOUGH*

I have written the book to resemble a training exercise or camp. The first five chapters are presented as if I were working with a player who had come to see me to improve on-ice performance. Usually, I begin the consultation by listening to the player describe his game. I ask about recent performances, his strengths, the areas he needs to develop, and his concerns. Then I discuss some basic principles of how the mind works and the importance of mind-body balance in creating the right performance state for hockey. These topics are covered in chapter 1.

In chapters 2 and 3, I explore how to maintain focus using both power thoughts (chapter 2) and high-performance imagery (chapter 3).

Maintaining right focus is difficult, if not impossible, if you are emotionally upset. In chapter 4, I discuss right feelings and how players can use breathing to release excessive tension, calm down, and maintain composure, as well as how to use breathing to energize and power up.

In chapter 5, I discuss a winning attitude. Specifically, I look at four elements of winning: commitment, confidence, identity, and love of the game. The chapter includes examples and suggestions for what a player (or coach) can do to bring these forces more into play.

Chapter 6 sheds some light on the mental qualities NHL scouts and coaches look for in young players. The chapter concludes with a discussion of hockey toughness.

Hockey is a team game, and team play is essential to team success. Chapter 7 discusses teamwork and the keys to becoming a more complete team player.

Chapter 8 discusses the importance of mental preparation and describes techniques that different players and different personality styles have found to be effective.

I recommend that anyone who plans to use the book as a training camp read through the entire book first, then go back and work on the chapters that interest you most. Chapters 1 through 8 have homework assignments. If your goal is to improve your game, then I recommend doing the assignments at the end of each chapter.

Chapters 9, 10, and 11 discuss scoring, playing defense, and tending goal. Each chapter contains insights from many experienced NHL players. Wherever possible, I relate their comments to the training suggestions presented earlier in the book.

Chapter 9 focuses on scoring and includes training suggestions from NHL scorers, including Markus Naslund, Pavel Bure, Alexander Mogilny, Paul Kariya, Steve Yzerman, Mark Messier, Luc Robitaille, and Cliff Ronning. Chapter 10 focuses on playing defense and includes tips from present and former NHLers Mattias Ohlund, Chris Pronger, Adrian Aucoin, Larry Robinson, and Kimmo Timonen, as well as checkers Bob Gainey, Brad May, Dave Scatchard, and Tiger Williams. Chapter 11 focuses on applying hockey tough training to the unique challenges of playing goal. The chapter includes the comments and advice of experienced NHL goalies and goalie coaches Glen Hanlon, Curtis Joseph, Garth Snow, Dan Cloutier, Andy Moog, and John Vanbeisbrouck.

Hockey is a physically aggressive game. Chapter 12 provides some mental training tips for preventing and recovering from hockey injuries and recharging for future games. The chapter concludes with a look at lifestyle choices that support consistent high-level on-ice performance.

The book concludes with a commentary on coaching youth hockey.

While writing this book, I spoke with many players, coaches, and scouts, all of whom shared their experiences and their insights about preparation, feeling, focus, and a winning attitude. Two things are clear from our discussions. First, people are different—there is no one prescription or technique that fits everyone. Second, whether they are a player or coach, whether they are interested in developing individual skills or winning teams, people seem to follow a two-step process to improve their game: assess and adjust.

Start by becoming more aware of your needs and circumstances and assessing yourself. Ask yourself, "Who am I?" (Or, in the case of a team, "Who are we?") "What's the situation?" "What has to be done for me (us) to improve and excel?" Then, adjust your technique or training to improve. When you're done, reassess.

Development in hockey—and in life—is a continuous process. Throughout the book, whether we are discussing self-talk, imagery, emotional control, or attitude, whether it's about playing forward, defense, or goal, the way to improve play is to be aware of your needs and circumstances, make the appropriate adjustment, then reassess. Becoming a more complete player is not just about practicing your strengths. Rather, it's directly proportional to your honest evaluation of your abilities and your willingness to do the necessary work on those parts of your game that you need to improve.

**CHAPTER**

**1**

# Managing the Mental Game

Success in hockey—and in life—is about learning to manage your mind effectively. By managing the mind effectively I mean setting clear, challenging goals; defining specific on-ice tasks; maintaining a positive focus; creating and using power thoughts and high-performance images; tuning out negativity, fear, anger, doubt, and distraction; creating empowering feelings; and nurturing a positive, winning attitude. All of these elements are building blocks to becoming hockey tough.

## WELCOME TO TRAINING CAMP

It's the beginning of training camp; a new season is about to begin. I'm standing in front of 40 prospective NHLers. The head coach is giving an enthusiastic talk to the rookies, telling them about the excellent opportunity that training camp offers. Indeed, ever since they were kids, many of these young athletes have dreamed of going to an NHL camp and making the team.

"Some of you will make the team this year," the coach says. "Some of you will play in the NHL in the next few years. Some of you will learn things in this camp that you will take with you and that will help you to be better players and better people." The coach goes on to describe the rules and regulations of training camp and then introduces me as the team's sport psychologist. As I get up to speak, I recognize a mix of curiosity, interest, and uncertainty on the players' faces. I pick up where the coach left off, talking about opportunity.

"This camp is an opportunity," I tell them. "And I believe the best way to take advantage of an opportunity is by managing your mind." I continue by underlining the importance of two mental skills that will help them play well.

First, *maintain a positive and productive focus throughout the camp.* For most of them, camp will be a new, pressure-filled experience. They will have many things to think about, but I encourage them to focus their thinking on the positive, especially where it applies to what they want to do on the ice. I tell them not to worry about what the coach is thinking. "Don't waste your time and energy wondering why the coach did or didn't put you on this or that line. Don't worry about whether he noticed what you did or didn't do on the last shift. Don't dwell on a poor play or a poor shift. You get more of what you think about, so stay focused on the positives." I tell them to concentrate on the things that got them here, things like moving their feet, passing tape to tape, playing the body, finishing checks, shooting accurately, and working hard.

Second, *learn to control feelings.* I explain a little bit about how feelings affect thinking and how breathing can be an important way to control those emotions that can interfere with performance. "Just taking a breath can help you to feel more calm and can control feelings like fear and anger that pop up." I mention how anxious feelings cause players to squeeze the stick, force the play, or wonder whether they should or shouldn't fight. These feelings are common at training camp because players want so badly to impress the coach.

I keep my comments brief because I know this is not the time for a detailed explanation or for any in-depth mental training. These young men want to get on the ice and play hockey. They are motivated to excel, to be great. They want to show what they can do. I will consult with them in greater depth later in the camp and during the season.

During the next week, I consult with several rookies individually. One of them, Ken, is a young defenseman who had an excellent training camp and exhibition season last year. He felt he should have made the NHL team but instead spent the season in the American Hockey League (AHL), where he played very well. I begin by asking Ken how things are going. He says that he's feeling good but acknowledges that he's nervous. He really wants to make a good impression. He wonders if there is something I can do to help him play with more confidence so he can have an even better camp than he did last year. I tell him that wanting to do well is admirable, but unchanneled emotion often leads a player to try too hard, which can be a hindrance. I ask Ken, "If you were a coach looking at a young prospect, what could he do that would impress you and indicate that he is ready to be on your NHL team?"

"Play with confidence," Ken replies.

"Okay, and how would you go about doing that?" I ask. "What specific things could you do on the ice that would give you a sense of confidence?"

"Well, I would skate well. Move the puck well, make good passes, finish my checks, and be strong in clearing the front of our net."

"Can you do these things at this level?"

"Absolutely," Ken replies.

I point out to Ken that it is important to have a clear, positive idea of what to do on the ice—and it sounds to me like he does. With that in mind, confidence comes from two things: having the right feelings, that is, believing in your ability to do the right things on the ice, and then actually doing them. I tell Ken that one thing he can do to build confidence is to visualize himself making the plays he has just described. We spend some time doing relaxation and visualization exercises. Ken goes on to have a good camp and by the end of November is playing a regular shift on the NHL club.

In the next 10 chapters, we'll describe the process that helped Ken and many other players sharpen their focus, manage their feelings, and build their confidence.

## MENTAL HOCKEY

How much of the game is mental? This is a good question and one I discussed with veteran NHL coach Roger Neilson. Roger told me that when he was with the Philadelphia Flyers, the team's sport psychologist put that very question to the players at a team meeting. "What percentage of the game do you think is mental?" he asked. "Raise your hand when I get to the percentage you think is the best answer." According to Roger, no one raised his hand at 30 percent, 40 percent, or even 50 percent. A few hands were raised at 60 percent and a few more at 70 percent, but most of the players raised their hands at 80 percent.

The question could be debated endlessly. Most athletes and coaches would agree that, given a certain level of physical ability, success in the sport is mostly mental. It relies on focus, determination, and emotional control, and it's the result of mind and body working well together.

Excellence in any sport is the result of the successful integration of physical, technical, and mental factors. However, in most sports, a disproportionate focus is put on the physical and technical aspects of training while mental training is relatively ignored. It's the same in hockey.

In 2001, I asked Doug Risebrough, a former NHL player and coach who is now the general manager of the NHL's Minnesota Wild, how he began the process of building a competitive hockey team. "First," he said, "select people of character. Choose guys who are winners, who want to win, and are willing to work together to make that happen." Doug added that resiliency is a key quality that goes hand in hand with being a winner. He also underscored the importance of players having a team goal and the ability to stay positive, focused, and to keep working hard, no matter what. Are focus, positive-mindedness, and resiliency qualities that can be learned and coached? I certainly think so.

## STIMULUS-RESPONSE

Psychology is the study of behavior. One way to study behavior is to break it down into stimulus and response units. A stimulus is something we perceive, something we see, hear, or think. A response is a way of reacting to what we perceive.

In sport, we are constantly surrounded by and bombarded with thousands of stimuli. To be effective in hockey, a player must be selective and focus on specific stimuli or cues. That's what we mean when we say a player makes good reads. Then he must respond to those stimuli in specific, effective ways. The whole process is instantaneous. For example, imagine a defenseman who is skating backward and watching the puck. He reads a two-on-one situation—a complex stimulus situation—and responds by positioning himself to take away the pass. The goalie reads the same stimulus situation and responds by playing the shooter and reacting to the movement of the puck. A critical part of success in hockey is a player's ability to read a situation, focus on the relevant stimuli or cues, and react quickly and appropriately.

Thinking can be both a stimulus and a response. A thought can stimulate action, yet can also be a response to something we have perceived. For example, a player can think about his role and responsibility—first man in on the forecheck takes the body—which is a stimulus for action, and respond by attacking the defenseman with the puck. Or he can think of his commitment to playing with discipline every shift (which is a stimulus) and respond by staying with his check rather than chasing the puck.

Now consider how thinking can also be a response. After a good shift, a player can say to himself something like "Good work. That's me. That's how I'm capable of playing." This is a thinking response that builds confidence. After a poor shift in which he left his man open in front of the net, a player can respond by thinking, "I can do better than that. That's not me. I always stay between my man and the net." Similarly, a player can read external (what's happening on the ice) or internal (feelings like fatigue and pain) stimuli and adjust his game accordingly.

Going into his third game in four nights, Joe, a tough rushing defenseman who played more than 25 minutes a game, was feeling sore and tired. After reading these feelings (internal stimuli), he adjusted by simplifying his game a little. Although he still played hard, he rushed less and focused more on his defensive responsibilities and being effective in staying closer to home.

## MANAGING YOUR MIND

The way you manage your thinking and feelings (your mind) is basic to how you perform. It's up to you. Improving your game begins with taking responsibility for managing your mind. I believe there are three key operating principles for managing the mind effectively.

The first principle is that the mind is like a TV set (figure 1.1). It's always on, thinking thoughts, running images, and creating feelings. What's important to understand is that you control the channel changer on that mental TV. You're the boss. You're in control. If you don't like what you're watching, if what you're watching doesn't give you power or doesn't feel good to you, then change the channel.

**Figure 1.1**   What's on your mental TV?

Being hockey tough is about your ability to stay on the power channel. My job as a sport psychologist is to show you two things: how to change channels on your mental TV and how to develop better quality programs to tune into.

The second principle of effective performance is that you get more of what you think about. Due to a mental phenomenon called *lateral inhibition,* whatever stimulus we focus on becomes magnified in our perceptual field while all other stimuli are downplayed. If you are worried and focus on thoughts and feelings that cause you anxiety (for instance, failure, embarrassment, pain, or disappointment), these thoughts and this reality will become magnified in your mind. Thinking thoughts such as "We're going to blow this lead," "This guy is impossible to check," "How am I supposed to play with these guys as my linemates?" or "I can't put the puck in the net" increases the likelihood of a negative performance.

Many players are negative thinkers. At a midget AAA team meeting, I asked a 16-year-old player how many shots he usually took in a game. After thinking a moment, he said, "Five or six." Then he added, "And I'll probably miss the net on all of them." With thinking like that, he's probably right.

You may say, "Well, he's just a kid." Larry Robinson, a perennial NHL all-star defenseman and a successful NHL coach, told me the pros are just as hard on themselves. "Too many guys [in the NHL] come off the ice and dwell on their mistakes," he says. "There's not enough focusing on the positive aspect of the game."

On the other hand, if you concentrate on the things you want to make happen on the ice (e.g., moving your feet, keeping your head up and on a swivel, passing tape to tape, going hard to the net, releasing quickly, shooting the puck, shooting accurately, keeping your stick on the ice, finishing your check, and clearing the front of the net), you will increase the probability of these things happening. Positive results will follow.

It's important to think positively and to put positive power programs on your mental TV. Sounds simple, yet few people are able to stay tuned into positive thoughts and feelings all the time. Experts tell us that we think 50,000 to 60,000 thoughts a day. For most people, more than 80 percent of their thoughts are negative or self-critical. Which brings us to our third principle.

The third principle is that feelings affect thoughts and thoughts affect feelings (figure 1.2). This explains why we sometimes get stuck on negatives even though we know we should think positively. It boils down to the way we're wired as human beings, the way our nervous systems work. Every time we have a feeling, a thought automatically goes with it. If the feelings you are experiencing are fear, pain, or uncertainty, the thoughts you'll think will tend to be stress-inducing and limiting. On the other hand, if you feel strong, energetic, and in control, your thoughts will be more positive and your confidence will grow.

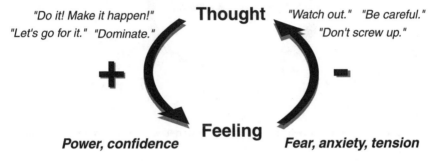

**Figure 1.2**  Feelings and thoughts are linked. How we think affects how we feel and how we feel affects how we think.

The feelings that most frequently limit hockey players have to do with fear, anger, frustration, fatigue, and pain. Figure 1.3 shows some examples of how negative feelings can affect thinking.

| Feeling | Thought |
| --- | --- |
| Fear (of failure) ➡ | "Don't make another mistake." "Don't screw up." |
| Fear (of injury) ➡ | "Watch out." "Be careful." |
| Anger ➡ | "I'm going to get him." |
| Frustration ➡ | "Something's wrong." "It's not happening." |
| ➡ | "There's no way." "What's the use?" |
| Fatigue ➡ | "I'm beat." "Not now, maybe later." |
| Pain ➡ | "Be careful." "Watch out." |

**Figure 1.3**  Negative feelings lead to negative thoughts.

Negative, limiting feelings can produce negative, limited thinking, which in turn feeds back more negative feelings, creating a negative loop that can become a trap (figure 1.4). That's exactly what a slump is all about: negative feelings, usually anxiety, producing and feeding negative thoughts that create more negative feelings.

**Figure 1.4** The loop of negative thoughts and negative feelings can lead to a slump.

Lou was a 30-goal-a-year scorer in the NHL. He told me that during those high-performance years, he went to the net with confidence and abandon. He felt strong, fast, and self-assured, and he just went for it. Then something unfortunate happened. As he drove to the net on a scoring chance, he was slashed across the face. The slash cut him badly and broke his jaw. After that injury, his feelings and focus changed. He lost some hockey toughness. He noticed he was tentative about going to the net. Instead of thinking, "I'll score," he began to think, "Watch out." He was looking to avoid a check as often as he was trying to put the puck in the net. As his feelings and focus changed, his goal production dropped dramatically and his career faltered.

Lou's scoring touch recovered as a direct result of his becoming a better mental manager and learning to change the channel on limiting feelings of fear—and the thoughts that go with fear—and replacing them with feelings and thoughts of power and impact.

Excellence in hockey, as in any sport, is a function of mind and body working together effectively. It's about smooth, coordinated function between thought and action. Excessive tension and fearful or negative thoughts cause a separation or disintegration of the mind–body unit that limits on-ice performance. The question is, how can we reduce these limiting negative thoughts and feelings? Understanding how the mind works and learning techniques to create powerful feelings and productive, positive thoughts will enable you to create a hockey tough state in which you can play your best.

# FOCUS AND FEELING

The hockey tough state is based on two things: focus and feeling. Your state is what you bring to any on-ice situation, whether it's in a game or in practice. You are responsible for your state. Most people think the word *responsible* means if you screw up or make a mistake, you're in for trouble. Actually, responsible means *response-able*. You are *response-able* for managing your mental TV. By that I mean you are *response-able* for creating the feelings and focus that will help you excel on the ice.

Being hockey tough involves taking *response-ability* for managing your mind in order to be the best you can be. To help you manage your feelings and focus your mental state, remind yourself to have a clear, positive focus, keep it simple, and use breathing to create right feelings and to change channels on your mental TV.

## Right Focus

Clear focus begins with clear goals. Goals help us direct our energy. I recommend that you set several types of goals, write them down, say them out loud, and repeat them to yourself frequently.

Set long-term or career goals. Some bantam and midget-age players (14- and 15-year-olds) I work with set personal career goals to play junior, collegiate, and even professional hockey. It helps to have a perspective that addresses why you play and where you want to go. You may set a goal to be the best player you can be, to make an elite team, or simply to enjoy the game.

Set goals for the season. Define what you want to achieve in terms of scoring, plus/minus, and team play. Then determine what you are going to do in terms of conditioning, skill development, and team play to make those goals a reality.

Set immediate goals for your next practice and game. For example, you may set a goal in practice to work on defending one-on-one, improving your shot from the point, or perfecting your skating. Setting practice goals and then doing the work is a good way to enhance skill development.

Last but not least, set team goals. Hockey is a team game. Team successes, both small and large, are paramount to a successful and enjoyable season.

Of course, goal setting is just the beginning. What's essential is that you realize what you have to do to accomplish your goals and then follow through. Once you've defined the basics, the ABCs, of what you want to do on the ice, it's time to do what's necessary in terms of conditioning, skill development, right focus, and hard work to execute those basics.

Being hockey tough is about having a clear direction, working hard, and following through. It's also about having a winning attitude. It's about being committed, confident, mentally tough or resilient, and having a passion for the game.

## Hockey Tough Focus

When I coach a player, I work with his focus and his feelings. I usually begin by asking what's happening in his game. How does he feel on the ice? More important, what would have to change for him to be at his best? The answer almost always involves a change in focus and in feelings.

Everyone is a performer. One of the first steps in developing more hockey toughness is being clear about your on-ice focus. You can use power thoughts and high-performance imagery to strengthen your focus and your ability to anticipate, react, and excel. In chapters 2 and 3, we'll look more closely at right focus and explore the thoughts and images that will help you do that.

When I asked Dave "Tiger" Williams, an NHL all-star and former client, if he thought sport psychology was useful, he said, "In my experience, it's another tool that a player can use to be better. When I played, they just trained the body, not the mind. Sport psychology can teach you how to focus. Many coaches tell you to focus, but many young athletes really don't know what that means." After reading this book, you will know.

# Right Feelings

Winning hockey is about managing feelings. Remember, our feelings affect our thoughts and our thoughts affect our feelings. You can't maintain right focus without managing feelings of fear, anger, pain, and fatigue. As I said earlier, you're the boss when it comes to how you think, feel, and act. You are *response-able*. Run positive programs on your mental TV and you will get more of what you think about.

Matt, an NHL all-star, told me a wonderful story of something that happened to him early in his career, before he achieved superstar status. Matt was playing for a coach who showed very little faith in his ability, who didn't play him much, and who treated him poorly. "The coach upset me so much that I couldn't even look at his face in the dressing room," Matt said. "Whenever he walked into the room, I had to look away." As Matt worked hard in the off-season preparing for the next season, he wondered and worried how he was going to deal with this unsupportive coach whom he perceived to be a huge negative obstacle in his hockey career.

Matt is a religious person with a strong faith. While participating in a Christian children's hockey camp during the summer, he was asked about his relationship with his coach. Matt couldn't lie. "I mentioned that this was one area of my game where I had a problem. Then I went on to talk about other things. Afterward one of the parents came over and spoke to me. She said, 'I really don't know you, but you seem to have a real problem with your coach. My suggestion is that you pray for him. It can change everything.'"

Matt said, "I remember thinking, the way that coach treated me and with my bad feelings for him, it would be very difficult for me to pray for him." Matt was desperate for things to change, however, so he followed the hockey mom's advice and began to pray for the coach. He said he prayed for the coach every day.

"It was interesting," Matt said. "After a little while, my feelings for the coach began to change. By the next season, the frustration and anger I had with the man had disappeared. At the start of the season, the coach didn't play me very much. He sat me for half the team's exhibition games. But it didn't bother me. I felt fine." Whenever he had a chance, Matt played well. Eventually, he was rewarded with more ice time. Relaxed and positive, he played better and better. Because of injuries to other players, Matt was moved to the first line and went on to have a career year. The following year Matt was an NHL scoring leader and was acknowledged as one of the best players in the game.

The key for Matt was taking responsibility for his situation and changing his thinking and feelings from anger, frustration, and negativity to tolerance and positivity. Reflecting on the experience, he said, "You can't play well when you're uptight, frustrated, and negative. You've got to find a way to focus on the positive. Prayer made the difference for me."

Not many hockey players or coaches would be willing to pray for those who upset them and treat them poorly. A more common response is anger, which perpetuates the existing feelings of *disease*. Shortly after I heard Matt's story, a minor hockey coach called to say he was having a real problem with some of the parents of the boys he coached. He mentioned one father in particular who was upset that his 14-year-old son wasn't getting the star treatment the father felt his son deserved. I knew the coach to be a fair and capable person who put a great deal of time and effort into providing his players with a very good hockey program. I mentioned the story Matt had told me and suggested that perhaps he should pray for the parent. He said, "Pray for that jerk? You've got to be kidding."

Matt's story highlights several of the keys to a winning mind that we outlined earlier. First, the mind is like a TV. If you don't like what you think or feel, it's up to you to change the channel. You are *response-able* for changing what's happening to you. Second, you get more of what you think about. Focus on how bad something or someone is and things are likely to get worse. Find a way to focus on something positive and empowering and things are more likely to move in a positive direction. Third, your feelings affect your thinking. Tense, angry, frustrated feelings usually lead to negative thinking, poor performance, and more negative feelings. Finally, attitude is a matter of choice. If you are confronted by a challenging, difficult situation, you always have a choice: either you use it or it'll use you.

Matt was a positive person. He chose to take responsibility, change his focus and his feelings, and use what was a very difficult situation for him. It paid off. It usually does.

I asked Stan Smyl, one of the Vancouver Canucks' all-time scoring leaders and now a successful coach, what he found useful about the sport psychology work we did together when he was a player.

He said, "I think it helps you to be more in control. It helps you to control your emotions as you prepare for games and even during a game. That's important, so you don't get too wound up and can think clearly and positively."

I agree with Stan's assessment. Winning hockey is about tuning into winning programs. It's about creating right focus and right feelings. We'll begin our training with right focus in chapter 2. In the meantime, there is one homework assignment for chapter 1.

# ASSIGNMENT: SETTING GOALS

Set your goals. As you begin reading this book, take the time to reflect on why you play hockey. What motivates you? What do you want to accomplish or achieve? It's very important to ask yourself these questions. The goals we set in hockey—and in life—come from our wants and desires. What do you want from the game?

Goals are about energy. They are desire channeled into direction. Your goals are a force you can use to energize your work habits, color your self-talk and imagery, and strengthen your attitude and team play. Research has shown that setting goals increases success. Take a few minutes to answer the following questions:

Why do you play hockey?

What do you want to achieve?

Do you have a long-term hockey goal? A career goal?

What is your goal for the season?

To achieve your season goals, you will have to work on your conditioning, skills, and ability to read the play and react.

What are your fitness goals for the season (for example, improvement in strength, aerobic capacity)?

What are your skill goals for the season (improvement in skating, shooting, passing, checking)?

List your mental strength goals for the season (for example, improvement in on-ice focus, pregame preparation, emotional control).

Team goals are important, too. After all, hockey is a team sport. List your team-play goals for the season (improvement in discipline, toughness, hard work, leadership). List a challenging and satisfying goal for your team to achieve this season.

Goals direct our energy. If you are clear that your goal is to be the best player you can be, then it's helpful to define a purpose or goal for each practice and game, something specific that you will work to improve. If you are unclear about something specific you want to work to improve, consult with your coach. Select a goal for your next practice. Select a goal for your next game.

Goals are a driving force. They are a way of putting desire to work. To make your goal a reality, you must get in touch with what you want to do and write it down. Read it, say it, and repeat it to yourself. Understand what you will have to work on to realize that goal, whether it's improving your skating, foot speed, physical strength, stick skills, or ability to read the game. Then get to work and persevere to make it happen.

Doing the homework is an important part of developing a winning hockey psyche. Make the effort to explore your goals now, and revisit them after reading the book, at the start of a new season, and at regular periods throughout the season.

# CHAPTER 2

# ┌─ Thinking in the ─┐
# └─ Power Zone ─┘

Players think all the time. The power thoughts you choose to focus on directly affect how you perform on the ice. Three kinds of power thoughts can be used to enhance your on-ice performance: strategy thoughts, feeling thoughts, and identity thoughts.

## STRATEGY THOUGHTS

The first kind of power thoughts is strategy thoughts. Simple strategies include keeping your eye on the puck and your feet moving. Of course, when it comes to reading the game and reacting well, there's more to it than just watching the puck and moving your feet. You have to make the right reads, anticipate the play, react well, and play the system. You can sharpen on-ice anticipation, judgment, and reactions by using strategy thoughts. For example, in a penalty kill situation, strategy thoughts for playing good defense might include maintaining good position and good angles, being aggressive but patient (don't commit), controlling the front of the net, and even keeping your head on a swivel and your stick active on the ice.

Being clear about what you want to do on the ice is basic to developing hockey toughness. That clarity can be reflected in a simple power thought. Indeed, your strategy thoughts should be so clear that just saying a thought to yourself brings to mind an image of that action. One way to organize your strategy thoughts is to define your job as **ABCs**. Your ABCs are the specifics of what you have to do on the ice to be effective. Let me give you two ABC examples.

Dave was a winger and a grinder with the Chicago Blackhawks. He worked very hard both to get a few shifts a game and to win the battles along the boards during those shifts. Because of his limited ice time, Dave worried about making the right impression on every shift. His problem was that he would try too hard, which limited his impact. I began working with Dave to increase his body awareness and help him relax. Then we reviewed Dave's ABCs. Dave was a big guy with a tendency to stand around at times and watch the play. He had to remind himself to keep his feet moving. Not surprisingly, thought **A** for Dave was to keep his feet moving. As a physical player, Dave had to use his size and strength to win the boards and finish his checks. Thought **B** was to win the puck on the boards. Dave also had to be sure to manage his defensive responsibilities—cover his check and get the puck out of his end. So Dave selected getting the puck out of his team's end as task **C**. Thereafter, whenever Dave worried about what the coach was thinking, he reminded himself to take a breath, remember his ABCs, and refocus on executing them. Being clear about what he had to do and focusing on doing it reduced Dave's anxiety and increased his impact.

**It really helps to take a breath and think about what you want to do out there.**

*David Legwand, center, Nashville Predators*

The second example is about Luke, a high-scoring NHL left winger. After a series of injuries and trades, he was acquired by the Los Angeles Kings. They gave him a chance to play on the power play. It was a high-pressure assignment that presented a real challenge. Luke knew that if he didn't produce, his career might be over. He was nervous.

After helping Luke relax, I asked him to list his ABCs, the three things he'd have to do to be successful on the power play. I told him his ABCs should be specific and clear enough that he could picture them. He thought for a moment, then listed his ABCs as getting the puck in his corner; making good passes, both to the center in the slot and to the point; and taking a good shot. When I asked if he could picture himself doing each of these ABCs, he answered that, yes, he could see it. "**A.** Get the puck in my corner. I'm like a cat pouncing on the mouse. **B.** Make good passes. I can see myself passing to the center in the slot and to the man at the point. I can even visualize who is playing these positions." He named the players. "**C.** Take a scoring shot. That's something I can feel in my hands more than visualize." Figure 2.1 illustrates Luke's power-play ABCs.

Curt Fraser, an NHL veteran and head coach, was asked what it takes to play in the NHL: "You have to know exactly what you want

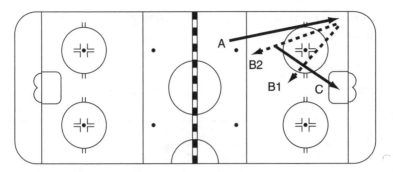

**Figure 2.1** Luke's power-play ABCs were to get the puck in the corner (A), make good passes to the center (B1) or the point (B2), and take an accurate shot (C).

to do in every zone and in every aspect of the game. You have to focus on the details."* These details are contained in your ABCs.

## Learning Your ABCs

**D**o you know your ABCs? They are an important key to developing and maintaining a clear, productive on-ice focus and playing winning hockey. They represent the specifics of what you should do in each situation. Create a clear thought and diagram for what you would do in each of the following situations.

What do you do when your team is attacking and has the puck in the other team's end?

A. _____

B. _____

C. _____

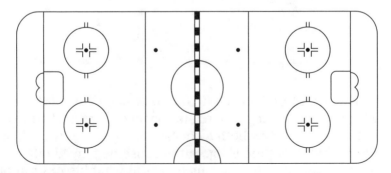

What do you do when you're defending and the other team has the puck in your end?

A. _____

B. _____

C. _____

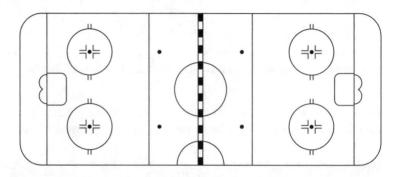

If you are on special teams, what do you do on the power play? When your team is killing a penalty?

A. _____

B. _____

C. _____

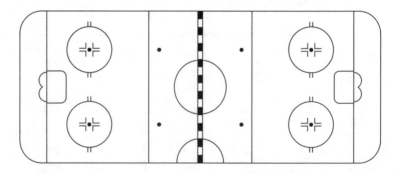

It's hard to be focused if you don't know your role. A veteran winger for the St. Louis Blues approached me after I had given a talk to the team. He was both a checker and a scorer with the Blues. I had talked about focusing, but because he played different roles on different lines, he was unsure about what his ABCs should be.

It was a hockey strategy question, one best answered by a coach, not a sport psychologist. However, understanding his uncertainty, I said to him, "You're an intelligent guy. It's important for you to be clear about your ABCs. And that's something that you really have to discuss with the coaching staff." He agreed to talk with them later and then left the room. As he did, one of the coaches approached me with a smile and said, "You know, Saul, I think that's the first time anyone ever told him he was intelligent."

I replied, "If you want him to play intelligent hockey, then you should tell him he is intelligent. And also help him to be clear about his ABCs."

Too often, coaches are critical of a player in a way that leads the player to think he's not smart and is incapable of playing intelligent hockey. Players will be more successful if they talk positively to themselves and focus on the specifics of what they want to do on the ice. Coaches will be more successful if they hold a positive image of a player's capabilities and focus on the specifics (the ABCs) they want the player to perform.

When you are coaching yourself or others, my ABC advice is that you define clear directions (ABCs) and know what you have to do on the ice, find positive things to acknowledge about your performance, and critique the behavior, not the person. By that last point I mean, if you're a coach and a player misses an assignment, don't run him down by saying, "You're stupid" or "What the hell is wrong with you?" Instead, provide the player with clear feedback about what he did—or didn't do—that was unacceptable and demand more. Tell him he is capable of better play. For example, say, "That's a poor decision. You're smarter than that. You're responsible for covering the front of the net. You know you don't go into the corner when there's no coverage in front of the net." Clear ABCs and positive power thinking are essential to increasing on-ice productivity.

In working with NHLers over the past two decades, I've had the chance to discuss the ABCs of scoring with many players (I relate some of their responses in chapter 9.). Not surprisingly, the one scoring power thought I heard repeated most often by scorers was "**A.** Shoot the puck."

## FEELING THOUGHTS

The second kind of power thoughts is feeling thoughts. These thoughts can help generate the feelings that give you an edge.

Examples of feeling thoughts include "good hands," "good wheels," and "good eyes." As you think a feeling thought, allow yourself to feel or experience it.

*Good hands* thinking can include "soft hands," "good touch," "the puck's on a string," or "snapping off quick, accurate shots and passes." Think these thoughts in practice and as part of your game preparation and feel them.

Examples of *good wheels* thinking include "feet moving," "feeling strong on my skates," and "I have good speed and good jump." Or it can include power skating thoughts such as "stay square," "low in the knees," "extend the stride," "full power, full length," and "turn and burn."

*Good eyes* thinking includes "head's up," "head on a swivel," "good reads," "anticipate," "know who's where," "find the open man," and "find the open space."

Another kind of feeling thought relates to intensity level. There's an optimal intensity level at which each player excels. Feeling too pumped, tight, and overaroused at one extreme or being too calm, flat, or laid back at the other can interfere with you playing at your best. This is especially true in an emotionally charged game like hockey. Learning how to create good feelings is important, and thinking is part of the process.

Under pressure, many players become tense, anxious, and try too hard. They may force the play, squeeze their sticks, chase the puck, retaliate, make mistakes, and compound errors. When this happens, a balancing thought is "smooth," which is effective when combined with doing the breathing and tension-release exercises described in chapter 4 to relax. On the other hand, if you are feeling low in energy, flat, and floating, then thinking "attack" can increase intensity and is often motivation to excel.

Moe was a scorer who found himself getting into foolish fights that took him off the ice. He was a high-intensity player with a low flash point. When he made a mistake or if someone hit him, he would get frustrated and angry and would overreact. The result was that he took thoughtless, selfish penalties that forced his team to work harder. Helping him to be calm wasn't simply a matter of explaining to him that a thoughtless reaction was selfish. To be able to manage his temper (and his intensity), Moe had to actually learn how to take a breath and think *smooth*. Affirmations such as "I'm a scorer, not a scrapper" were also helpful. I'll say more about affirmations later in this chapter.

Rick Lanz was a defenseman with the Vancouver Canucks and Toronto Maple Leafs in the mid-1980s when Wayne Gretzky was at his peak. I asked Rick, now an experienced hockey coach, what made Gretzky so effective. He said, "It was his ability to be calm (smooth) under pressure. He could hold the puck and take a look. When he'd do that, he would force you to make the first move."

I asked Markus Naslund, a leading goal scorer in the NHL, about his composure with the puck. Along with the need to work hard to get into scoring situations, Markus talked about the importance of patience—the ability to hold the puck and make the defenseman and goalie make the first move. These abilities come with experience and a way of thinking.

Thinking and feeling *smooth* can add to your on-ice intelligence and finish. Thinking and feeling *attack* can generate hustle and opportunity. Excellence is about finding a balance, and you're the boss. Learn when to *attack* and when to be *smooth*.

# IDENTITY THOUGHTS

Identity thoughts describe the way a player thinks about himself. They reflect a general sense of confidence and self-image. All-star center Mark Messier once told me, "A lot of players don't know anything about self-talk and the power of positive thinking. They don't realize that saying negative things to themselves, even when they are not playing, can lead to more negative play."

Someone in a difficult situation who thinks "I'm OK" and "I can handle it" is using positive identity thoughts. Some other positive examples are when someone under pressure thinks "I love a challenge" or when someone in an uncertain situation thinks "I (we) can work this out." This kind of thinking develops over time with positive life experiences. Think power, position, and impact to get more of what you think about. Identity thoughts can be nurtured by talking positively to yourself and using affirmations.

## Affirmations

Affirmations are simply positive statements you say to yourself, words that give you strength. Remember, you get more of what you think about. Affirmations are thoughts such as "I'm the boss," "I'm in control," "One shift at a time," "I read the play well," "I control the front of the net," and "I have a great goal-scoring reflex." A good affirmation for goalies is "I can stop everything I see."

I frequently make tapes for athletes in which I combine instructions for relaxation with power thoughts. On the tape, I remind the player to take a breath after each thought. I also point out that thought precedes action, so players should think positively, and that repetition builds strength, so players will get the best results by thinking these thoughts repeatedly.

To choose thoughts that will work well for you, explore how you want to feel and what you want to achieve. Once you've completed these two steps, create an affirmation or power thought that you feel comfortable saying to yourself. These statements should be credible to you and positive. The following is a list of affirmations that I prepared for Los Angeles Kings players. They were encouraged to select 6 to 10 power thoughts from the list and incorporate them into their self-talk.

I'm the boss (of my mental TV).

I make a difference every shift.

A little adrenalin and some breathing are like jet fuel.

I am *attack* and *smooth*.

I am quick and strong like a cat (tiger, panther, wolf).

I am strong on my skates.

I have great jump.

I am an accurate shot.

I have a great goal-scoring reflex.

I love to score goals.

I am a tough, aggressive checker.

I am unbeatable when I play the body.

The more I hit, the sharper I get.

I enjoy a challenge. I enjoy checking the great ones.

I am a winner. We are winners.

I am committed. I am willing to do whatever is necessary to achieve our goal.

My mind is a force I use to make things happen.

I am mentally tough.

I get stronger, tougher, and sharper with each shift.

## Choosing Affirmations

**R**eview the list of affirmations and determine which ones might work for you. Select those that are credible to you, that address your strengths or aspects of your game that you want to develop, or that just feel good to you. Select 6 to 10 affirmations or power thoughts that would most help you become a tougher, more positive, effective player. Or you can make up your own affirmations using the Kings' list as a reference. Write down your affirmations and say them to yourself often.

Affirmations can be in the first person ("*I* am smooth," "*I* am a power machine"), a format that is personal and powerful. Or you can affirm in the second person *("You* are a star," "*You* use everything"). In our day-to-day lives, other people usually address us in the second person. It's effective and pleasant to hear positive things said about us in the second person. I often make tapes for athletes repeating affirmations in both ways.

Words are like food for the spirit. They can nurture us. Just as you would choose to eat foods that you like or that are good for you, part of being a more effective player is saying things to yourself that feel good to you and that give you power.

Repetition builds strength. In the weight room, repetition of a simple physical exercise builds muscle power. It's the same with affirmations and power thoughts. Repeat your power words and thoughts to yourself frequently. Develop your positive mental focus and attitude. Whether you're relaxed or facing a challenge, take a breath and affirm the positive. Remember, choose power thoughts that create a feeling and a picture that increase your confidence, direction, and sense of what is possible.

Linda had been a hard-working winger on a national championship collegiate team. I spoke with her as she was preparing for a training camp in the women's professional hockey league. She described herself as a solid checker. When I asked her about her offensive prowess, she said, "I can score in practice, but not in games."

I pointed out to Linda the importance of being aware of her self-talk and maintaining a positive focus. I asked her to consider what she had just said about herself. "It may be that you are more of a checker than a scorer. However, if you want to develop your scoring ability, it's crucial that you change the way you talk and think about yourself." I told her, "I'm not suggesting that you see yourself stick-handling through the other team like Forsberg or Gretzky, turning on the jets and blowing past the defense like Bure or Kariya, or shooting like MacInnis or Hull. However, you are strong on the boards. Visualize yourself winning the puck on the boards and working the give-and-go. See yourself making the pass to the center high in the slot or to the point, then skating to the net, getting the pass, and shooting and scoring."

I told Linda to talk to herself using affirmations such as: "The puck is mine. I win the puck on the boards. I execute the give-and-go effectively. I have a good shot from in close. Scoring is just part of me working hard." "Affirm and imagine these abilities," I told her. "Practice the give-and-go off the boards and work on your shot in practice. Be a positive self-talker. Be a more complete player. Be a checker *and* a scorer."

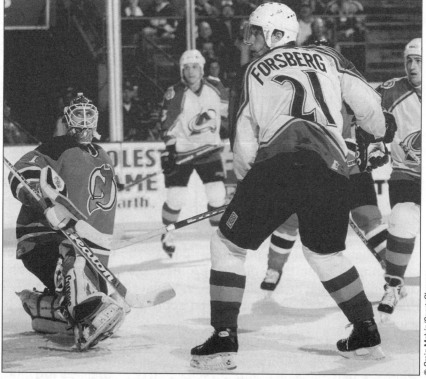

© Craig Melvin/SportsChrome

You don't have to see yourself as Peter Forsberg. Focus on maximizing your strengths.

John was a young player who admitted to playing poorly when his father came to the rink to watch him. He said his dad was a stern critic who always focused on what he did wrong. Just his being there made John feel uptight. I told John that his problem was not uncommon. I've seen players at every level, including the NHL, become unfocused trying to impress a parent or coach. I told John that the best antidote to the *dis-ease* of having a critic watch you play and wait for you to make a mistake is to be clear about what you want to do and be positive in talking to yourself.

Kenny was a defenseman who was struggling to make the Edmonton Oilers. He came to see me prior to his second training camp. He described having had a terrible training camp the previous season because, as he put it, "I was totally focused on what the coach was thinking instead of on my own positive thoughts. I was worried all the time. I wondered if the coach had seen me make that pass, if he saw me lose my check. I wondered why he changed my defense partner. I worried about everything. Bottom line, I was a nervous wreck. Instead of being positive and focusing on my job on the ice, I was focusing on what was going on in the coach's head. I didn't play well. And I don't want to repeat that situation." We started out by working on his breathing. Then I reminded Kenny to start thinking, "I'm the boss" and "I'm a star." He came to see himself as someone with good wheels, good hands, and good eyes. Then he defined his on-ice ABCs. Finally, he affirmed that he could execute his ABCs effectively and confidently. He repeated thoughts such as the following: "A. I make good reads and I maintain good position." "B. I'm strong and smart. I clear the front of the net. The front of the net is mine." "C. I make good passes and I get the puck out of our end."

I told Kenny, "You're an intelligent guy with an active mind. That's a plus. To become mentally tougher, anytime you have a worrisome thought, use it to remind yourself to take a breath and focus on your positive ABCs. Think positive. You get more of what you think about." He did, and he had a great camp.

When should you use positive thoughts? All the time. When you are aware of a negative thought, change it to a positive power thought. Remember, you get more of what you think about. Positive thinking works.

Some players report that being too thoughtful immediately before and during a game slows them down. They prefer to be in the moment, to react and create. Others have found that repeating ABCs and affirmations before a game increases focus and confidence. Define your ABCs. Create some power thoughts. Then find out, based on your experience, when doing mental reps works best.

## Power Statements

In addition to power words and thoughts, some players have used power statements to improve their game.

Al was a talented rushing NHL defenseman. He explained that over the long season, there were nights when he felt flat, dull, and unsure of himself and it was a struggle to get up for a game. He asked if there was something he could do to help prepare for the game and be sharper and more positive. First, I showed him how to use his breathing to feel more energized and powerful. Then we reviewed his ABCs and did some mental rehearsal. He visualized himself making all the plays. Last, we defined the following power statement:

### Al's Power Statement

- I am an outstanding hockey player.
- I am strong and fast and I read the play well.
- On offense, I have the ability to make things happen.
- I see opportunities and I make excellent passes.
- I have a strong, accurate shot.
- I have good wheels. I rush the puck with speed and confidence.
- I am a force when I jump into the play.
- I love to set up and score goals.
- On defense, I always have good position.
- I keep people to the outside.
- I move people from the front of the net.
- One-on-one, I am unbeatable.
- I am like a big cat, a tiger. I'm quick, strong, and powerful.
- I am intense and focused like a tiger hunting.
- I am quick. I react with my speed and power.
- Offensively and defensively, I am a force.
- I prepare myself well.

- I am a team player.
- I am composed. I don't let criticism bother the tiger. I use it.
- I enjoy playing this game and I am very good at it.
- I am an outstanding player.

Al's power statement consisted of a series of power thoughts and affirmations that reflected the best of Al's play. I encouraged him to memorize the statement and repeat it to himself before—not during!—each game. I suggested he take a breath after each thought and see himself performing well. Al was encouraged to do several reps of his power statement at a time. Remember, repetition builds strength.

The power thoughts you repeat in your power statement should make sense to you. They are a combination of your strengths and what you aspire to. For example, if you have a hard shot and are working on making it more accurate, you could say, "I have a hard, accurate shot." But if you don't skate particularly well, it would not be truthful or useful to say, "I have great wheels." It would be more effective to say, "I keep my feet moving. I anticipate the play and react quickly." As you work on your skating, tell yourself, "My foot speed is improving" and "I am getting quicker and faster."

Dennis was a talented young forward, a college all-star just breaking into the NHL. He had great wheels and soft hands. The rap on Dennis was that at times he simply wasn't aggressive or determined enough. Part of helping him increase his hockey toughness and follow-through was to show him how to use his breathing to pump up and be more centered. Another part of our mental training involved using the following power statement:

### Dennis's Power Statement

- I am an aggressive, hard-working player.
- I make things happen.
- I have great wheels.
- I take the puck to the net with speed and confidence.
- I am a scorer. I love to score goals.
- I have good hands.
- I work hard for the puck and I have great finish.
- I have a hard, accurate shot and I score.

- I have good eyes. I see opportunities, and I make excellent passes.
- I am a reliable defensive player.
- I always have good position.
- I am quick and smart.
- I am like a panther hunting—always moving, eyes open, ready to strike.
- I am unstoppable.
- Every game, I am physically and mentally ready to play.
- I am tough. I play hard every shift.
- I am a team player.
- I enjoy playing this game and I am very good at it.
- I am an aggressive, hard-working player.

Like Al, Dennis was encouraged to repeat each thought in his power statement slowly to himself before games. After each statement, he was encouraged to take a breath, see it happening, and then go out on the ice and make it happen.

## Writing a Power Statement

Prepare your own power statement. Write out a statement of who you are (or could be) at your best. Affirm all of your strengths and highlight your potential. If there is a quality that you could have manifested but haven't as yet, incorporate it into your power statement. Read this statement to yourself. Repeat it often. Let it become you.

Assess and adjust. You need to become aware of who you are and what you need to do to excel. Many players have reported that they have found the ABCs and the power statements helpful as focusing and mind-strengthening tools and useful components of their pregame preparation. Others have said that the less they think about hockey right before a game, the better they play. Regardless of pregame preferences, everyone can benefit from running positive (instead of negative) programs on their mental TV. The programs you choose are personal. Increase your mental strength. Create and use power thoughts, self-talk, and affirmations that meet your needs and circumstances and feel right to you.

# HOMEWORK

## Assignment 1: Defining ABCs

A key part of your on-ice focus is to have a clear sense of your role on the ice in a variety of situations. Define your ABCs in each of the following situations that are relevant to you.

Your team is breaking out of your end:

A. _____

B. _____

C. _____

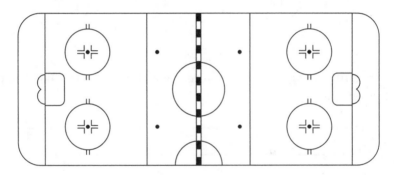

Your team has the puck in the opposing team's end:

A. _____

B. _____

C. _____

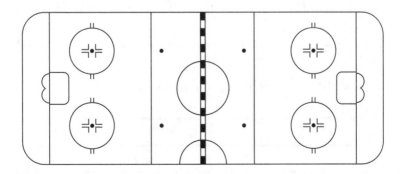

Your forechecking scheme is:

A. _____

B. _____

C. _____

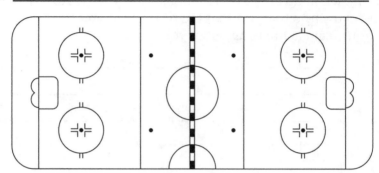

The opposing team is moving toward your end or has the puck in your end:

A. _____

B. _____

C. _____

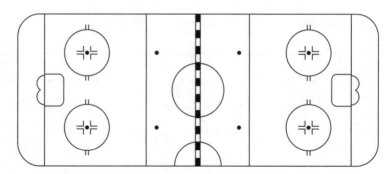

Special teams: You are on the power play:

A. _____

B. _____

C. _____

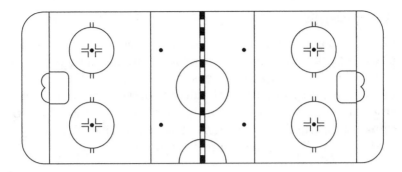

Special teams: You are killing a penalty:

A. _____

B. _____

C. _____

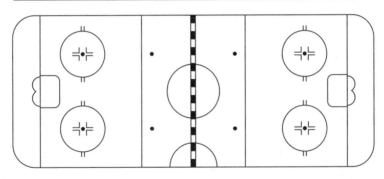

## Assignment 2: Affirmations and Power Thoughts

Select 6 to 10 affirmations or power thoughts. Repeat them daily: in the morning, before stepping out onto the ice, between shifts, and after a game. Some people tape a list of their favorite affirmations to the mirror and look at themselves while repeating them. Give it a try.

## Assignment 3 (Optional): Power Statement

Create a power statement that describes you and how you play at your best. Repeat it to yourself often and imagine yourself performing at that level.

## Assignment 4 (Optional): Positive Reading

We are what we think. There are many books that highlight the power of positive thoughts, as well as biographies of highly successful athletes and achievers in all walks of life. One way to become a more positive thinker and performer is to become a student of positive thought and read about the impact of positive thinking on the lives of others. Read a positive biography in the next month, then pass it on to a teammate.

# CHAPTER 3

# Imaging With Impact

I'm often asked if I use imagery to help my clients perform better. I certainly do! Imagery is basic to high performance. Most of the athletes I work with have used some form of imagery on their own before I ever coached them on the process.

Does imagery work? Yes. Research has shown that athletes who mentally rehearse their performance perform significantly better than those who don't. This is particularly true with regard to accuracy. I have worked with athletes in more than 25 different sports and have seen major-league pitchers, pro golfers, basketball players, and Olympic sharpshooters use imagery rehearsal as an accuracy-enhancing tool. Hockey players can also improve their shooting accuracy and other skills with mental rehearsal.

Longtime NHL coach Mike Keenan likes to say, "The ability to visualize is one of the most valuable psychological abilities a player has to prepare himself to play and improve his performance." That's not to say imagery training was or is the norm. Tiger Williams once told me, "I don't think many guys do it. They may think about wanting to score on the bus on the way to the game, but they don't imagine the actual skating, shooting, and checking that makes it happen. And as for coaches teaching it, they don't. At least it never happened to me, and I played for a dozen coaches in the macho pro atmosphere of the NHL."

Times appear to be changing, however. Recently Chris Pronger, the Norris Trophy-winning captain of the St. Louis Blues, told me, "I think most players do some visualization. I visualize myself making the plays and doing positive things on the ice. Visualization helps me to get into the right frame of mind."

Essentially, I use four kinds of imagery with hockey players: mental rehearsal, imagining the successful end result, stimulating images, and recharging images.

# MENTAL REHEARSAL

Mental rehearsal means actually visualizing and practicing in your mind the things you want to do on the ice. This includes mentally rehearsing both your on-ice skills and your responses to game situations (ABCs).

Mentally rehearsing on-ice skills includes imagining; seeing or feeling yourself skating with speed, power, and jump; handling the puck skillfully and with confidence; passing tape to tape; shooting the puck accurately; scoring; and finishing your checks.

Mentally rehearsing your response to game situations involves visualizing yourself making good reads and executing your ABCs. In the case of Luke, the left-winger we discussed in chapter 2 (page 16), it means

A. imagining or seeing himself going into the corner and getting the puck "like a cat on a mouse";

B. imagining himself making a crisp, accurate pass to the center in the slot or the man at the (left) point; and

C. experiencing the feeling of snapping a quick, hard, accurate wrist shot into the net.

## Fifty Goals a Day

I have suggested to many of my clients that they score a minimum of 50 goals a day. By that I mean they visualize the goal and then imagine shooting a puck into the net and scoring 50 imaginary goals a day. I even took a photo of a hockey goal, had it blown up to approximately three by four feet, and gave out the enlargements to players to put on the walls of their bedrooms and use as the target for their imagery practice. It worked well, except that several players decided to actually shoot pucks at the wall. Although that may have improved their on-ice performance, it certainly didn't please their landlords.

Brad was an NHL winger who struggled with scoring. When I visited his home, I noticed that he had a lovely large fireplace in his living room. "This is perfect," I said. He looked puzzled. "You should score 50 goals in this fireplace every day. And when you do, pick your corners. Put five in the top left corner. Then visualize five in the top right corner, then five bottom left, and so on. Sharpen that mental image. Practice on the ice. You'll see, when you get those two or three scoring opportunities in a game, the puck will start going in for you."

Many players practice mental rehearsal before games. Cliff Ronning told me that Marian Gaborik, the young scoring sensation for the Minnesota Wild, sharpens his offensive finish on game day by visualizing himself making quick moves, going to the net, firing into the corners, and scoring.

Research suggests that for best results, combine mental rehearsal with on-ice practice. When Stanley Cup-winning coach Terry Crisp was coaching the Soo Greyhounds of the Ontario Hockey League, he told me that he would occasionally have his players imagine themselves one-timing a crossing pass into the net, just as they would run the drill in practice, only without the puck. He thought it was beneficial. Years later, Terry confided that when he was a player, NHL master coach Fred Shero made him do an on-ice drill designed to increase shooting and accuracy in which he would actually skate down the wing and shoot an imaginary puck at the goal. Mental rehearsal is like a blueprint that strengthens and clarifies intent and, in doing so, increases the probability of success.

## Learn to Imagine

One of the best ways to begin practicing mental rehearsal is to imagine yourself playing hockey with confidence and effectiveness in a situation in which you have been successful in the past. First, take a couple of breaths. Most of my clients have found that relaxing and breathing improves the quality and clarity of their imagery. Now see yourself on the ice. Imagine feeling good, skating with strength and smoothness, seeing the whole ice surface, and handling the puck with composure and confidence.

Begin your imagery with things you do easily. Then gradually imagine performing well in more difficult or challenging aspects of the game. If you are a goalie, see and feel yourself having good position, seeing shots clearly, feeling quick, and handling all shots with confidence. First, imagine a single shooter crossing the blue line and taking a shot. You have good position and handle it easily.

Next, imagine the shooter moving in closer to the top of the circle and shooting. Again, you have good position and see the puck clearly and stop it cleanly, without a rebound. Imagine two-on-ones: playing the shooter, making the save, then playing the pass and coming across quickly and under control to make the save again. Run through a complete warm-up in your mind, imagining yourself maintaining good position, staying square, challenging, being sharp and quick, playing at your best, making all the saves and controlling the rebounds. If you'll be facing a team with players who have an unusual move or shot, mentally rehearse yourself reacting well and making the save against them.

---

*Repetition builds strength.* Repeatedly practicing mental rehearsal will help develop both your imagination and your on-ice skills so that you will be better able to read, anticipate, and react in any situation.

Mental rehearsal is useful in all aspects of the game. On offense, imagine yourself skating well, making good passes, jumping into the play, keeping your feet moving, winning battles on the boards, getting open, going hard to the net, shooting accurately, and scoring. On defense, visualize yourself skating well, reading the play, picking up your check, maintaining good position, angling your guy to the outside, playing the body, pinning him against the boards, clearing the front of the net, and getting the puck out of your end.

*Mentally rehearse your ABCs.* Visualize yourself in the offensive zone with the puck; see the breakout, picture yourself coming back hard and angling your check to the boards in transition, and visualize your ABCs on defense, on the power play, and on the penalty kill. In each situation, visualize yourself executing the play perfectly.

Don't forget to mentally rehearse difficult situations. It can be helpful on occasion to imagine how you would handle things going wrong and on-ice events that you can't control, such as the referee missing the call, scoring a goal that is disallowed, an unexpected delay in the game, or having your role or line changed. In each instance, imagine maintaining composure, taking a breath, staying focused on the positive, and playing good hockey.

## Tips for Creating a Winning Hockey Movie

Imagery is like a movie, and you are the director. Creating and experiencing your own high-performance hockey movies will help you excel. Here are seven tips that will enhance your mental rehearsal.

*1. Visualize your ABCs.* Uncertainty leads to confusion and nervousness. One way to increase success and reduce stress is to create clear images of your ABCs. Stay tuned into these images. Be specific. Project your energy into the images of what you want to create on the ice.

*2. Relax and then image.* Whenever possible, relax and take a breath before putting your imagination to work for you. As you do, the quality of your thoughts and images will become stronger, clearer, and more positive. Take a few minutes before the game to relax and imagine performing at your best. In hockey, that may mean being faster, more powerful, being strong on your skates, making good reads, finishing checks, and having soft hands, more patience, and excellent stick-handling, passing, and shooting skills.

Not everyone finds relaxation performance enhancing. I made a relaxation and imagery tape for Dale, an NHL power forward who wanted to enhance his scoring with some mental rehearsal. When I followed up with him to get his response to the tape, he said, "I like the imagery part; that helps. But the relaxation makes me too relaxed." My advice to him was to only do the imagery. Above all, do what works for you.

*3. Stay positive.* You get more of what you think about and imagine. Stay focused on the image of you at your best. The only value in running a negative image of something that didn't work—getting beat one-on-one, missing an open net, letting in a soft goal—is to determine what you can do to make that play the next time. Then mentally rehearse the positive.

*4. Go easy at first.* As a general rule, it's best to move from what is easy to what is more challenging. This is true in mental as well as physical training. When you first begin, see and feel yourself handling simple situations with confidence. For a goalie, that could mean starting mental rehearsal by stopping long shots from the blue line that can be seen clearly. Then make the imagery more challenging—two-on-ones, breakaways, power-play pressure, and lots of in-close puck movement in front of the net.

*5. Be dynamic.* Most athletes find imagery works best if they imagine themselves playing from the perspective of the player on the ice. Others have had success visualizing performance as if they were a spectator in the stands watching themselves perform. Try both approaches and see what feels and works best. Many players find slow-motion imagery very helpful, especially for improving skill moves. Others prefer to do mental rehearsal in real time at game speed.

6. *Be brief.* You can benefit by imagining 5- to 10-second flashes of making a pass, jumping into the play, getting a rebound and finishing, or taking the body and finishing a check. You don't have to imagine a whole shift.

7. *Use all your senses.* Make your mental rehearsal multisensory. Most people are strongly visual, and many think imagery is simply visual. Hockey has very strong visual, tactile, and kinesthetic elements. You may get the best results by using any or all of the sensory cues—see it, feel it, hear it, and when appropriate, smell it and taste it. Some players have said they prefer to feel themselves shooting well as opposed to seeing it.

There is no absolute right time or right way to rehearse mentally. Some players do it the night before a game, some the afternoon of a game, some a few minutes before a game, and some not at all. Some players use images that relate directly to the team they are facing in the upcoming game. For others, mental rehearsal is more generic and focuses on making plays and executing good skills, regardless of the opposition. Experiment and discover what works best for you.

Donald Brashear, an NHL player and policeman, underscores the importance of mental preparation and specifically mental rehearsal in helping him maintain control. He told me, "The main thing I do to keep control is visualize before the game what's going to happen and how the game is going to unfold. I think about what kind of players they have and which guys are going to be thrown at me. The main thing is anticipation. You need to anticipate what might be thrown at you so your reactions are natural when you get into the game. That way, when something happens, you know what to do right away." Donald continued, "It's the same with scoring a goal. You imagine you have the puck in a certain type of situation. You visualize it happening. Then, when it comes to you in the game, your reaction is natural."

I asked Donald how he deals with different challenges from players mouthing off and trying to get him to fight. He responded, "There are different situations. It depends on the type of player doing it. If it's a tough guy who's bugging me, there's a matter of respect. If he's doing it to me and I don't respond, then I know he's going to be doing it to some other player, so I have to take control and show him right away. But if it's a smaller player, I know he's not going to want to drop his gloves. He may be just trying to get me to take a penalty. Being in control requires a lot of focus, a lot of work with your mind before the game, and also the day before the game. I think about it a lot. You also have to consider the circumstance in the game, who's winning, and whether your team needs a lift. I have started fights at times when it woke up the other team and gave them a lift. Obviously, that's not good. So you have to consider many things and prepare yourself well in advance."

# IMAGINE THE SUCCESSFUL END RESULT

A second kind of imagery that enhances performance is to think about the successful end result you want to achieve. Create and hold the image of exactly what it is you are working toward, whether it's playing professional, college, or junior hockey, making the school or AAA team, making the playoffs, or winning the championship.

Most sport psychologists believe that it's more important to think of the process of how you are going to get there (that is, mental rehearsal) than it is to focus on the end result. I agree. However, clarifying intent by having a clear end-result image can mobilize a process that puts powerful unconscious forces to work for you. It can also sustain you and help you endure the rigors of training necessary to get you where you want to go.

When I discussed imagery with Steve Yzerman, he said, "At night, I definitely lie there and dream about holding the Stanley Cup or scoring a big goal. It's something you just do about things you care about."

Visualize yourself playing on an NHL or national team or at the junior, college, school, AAA, or rep level. This image may help you sustain the drive to reach your goal. Putting a photograph on the wall of yourself (or a favorite player or role model) scoring or making a big save, or being a part of a team that you aspire to, can motivate and support you in getting where you want to go.

A junior hockey player reported that looking at a photo of Canada's gold-medal Olympic hockey team when he woke up each morning sparked him to get up and out of bed early and to the gym for his summer workout. A success image is no substitute for the effort needed to succeed, but it can energize and sustain you through the long hours of training necessary to get there.

## Choose Your Image

Choose an end result and put a relevant picture up on the wall. Use the picture to remind you of what you are working to achieve and why the training and consistent effort that you put in are important. Let that image become a source of energy to support you in maintaining your efforts.

## STIMULATING IMAGES

The third kind of imagery I use to help athletes excel is one that some hockey players have found to be useful and many have found to be fun. I often ask the question, "If you had to pick an animal that would give you qualities you want to have on the ice and would help you play winning hockey, which animal would you choose?" The animals most hockey players select are the big cats: tigers—panthers, lions, leopards, and jaguars. Some defensemen have picked bears.

The idea is that each of us is a combination of an animal with a strong, powerful physical body, as well as strong emotions and feelings, and an angel. The angel part of our being enables us to use our thoughts and images to create and shape our reality. The animal part relates to our emotions, heart, physical strength, and energy.

You can use imagery to awaken the animal spirit within you. The reason many players use imagery of the big cats is that they have tremendous power, balance, and speed. They are brave and aggressive. They are crafty and smart. They play their angles perfectly. They love to hunt and they never worry. If their prey eludes them, they don't sulk or ruminate about it. And unlike some hockey players I have known, they don't run themselves down or get depressed if they have a poor shift, if they haven't scored in a couple of games, or if they let in a soft goal.

Bret Hedican is one of the most mobile defensemen in the NHL. He is also a very motivated athlete and an excellent team player who was willing to explore how sport psychology training could enhance his game. Bret says that what helped him most in our early sessions was learning how to relax and stay composed. "In wanting to play well, I sometimes tried too hard, which was at times counterproductive. After mastering the relaxation and breathing, one of the things that's helped me most is imagery, specifically the image of a jaguar," he said. "Sometimes I imagine myself as a jaguar hunting, being low on the ice, having good vision, knowing who's on the ice, where they are, and being ready to react quickly."

Bret went on to say, "I think of myself as a jaguar, unaffected by stresses and negatives, by good shifts or bad shifts, or the press. If we have back-to-back games and I'm tired, I hunt smarter. I have learned to assess my energy level. And, like an animal, when I'm tired, I use my energy better. I'm wiser and more patient. I stay back in the weeds a little more when I'm hunting."

Val was a veteran on an NHL team that was struggling. He was a big, strong, experienced player and a popular, outgoing teammate whom everyone liked and many younger players looked up to. However, Val's work ethic was mediocre. I explained that because of his experience, size, and presence, his teammates noticed him, and many, especially the younger players, looked to him for leadership whether he asked for that or not. I related that when he didn't appear to be giving 100 percent, it was noticed and mirrored by others.

We spoke about increasing his intensity. I told Val that he was like a lion: big, strong, and powerful. It was important to the team that he realize his potential, fire up the lion within him, and become a tougher, more focused, and aggressive competitor. He understood. More important, he liked the image and used it to lift his game.

Your animal image should represent you at your best. It's you at your physically strongest, with sharp reflexes, quick reactions, great balance, power, and jump. By selecting the tiger or panther, you can identify with a power source with great courage and heart, with superhuman quickness and speed, with strength and power and remarkable reflexes, that can attack and hunt with efficiency. Animal images can provide power and heart.

When you think cheetah, tiger, or jaguar, or whatever animal image you choose, allow it to awaken that animal in you. Allow it to stimulate you to turn the wheel. Turning the wheel fires up the tiger. It awakens your speed and jump and power.

Several defensemen have selected bears rather than big cats. I asked Jeff, a veteran of the NHL and the International Hockey League, what appealed to him about being a bear. He pointed to two qualities: size and power. He described how, as a bear, he could visualize himself going into the corner and overpowering his man or being an immovable force in front of the net. He reminded me that bears are not just strong, but they're also very quick. Several wingers chose wolverines for their aggressiveness and tenacity (and they weren't all from the University of Michigan).

If you are going to use animal imagery and call on the energy and spirit that's there, you have to do the training necessary to support it.

## Identify Your Animal

Select the image of an animal that appeals to you. Think about turning the wheel, generating power, and firing up the animal within. Whether you are under pressure, tired, and have low energy or are dominating, use the situation you are in to stimulate you to turn the wheel and energize the animal, then think ABCs and hunting.

# RECHARGING IMAGES

Hockey is a physically and mentally demanding game. On the ice, players are expected to give 100 percent. Off the ice, you should have a way to recharge. I discuss recharging imagery in depth in chapter 12. For now, I simply want to underscore that you can use imagery to prepare for, focus, and intensify your game and to relax, recharge, and get ready for the next one.

As always, assess and adjust. Develop images that work for you. Combining images with right feelings and power thoughts is very effective. Imagery can be a powerful aid to your preparation and on-ice performance. It can also help you develop a more positive, high-performance attitude.

# USE ACTUAL VIDEO TO ENHANCE PLAY

Many teams have coaches who analyze video of games and break it down so that the players can use it to prepare for games and develop their skills. I have also seen coaches tape practices and then review a player's performance when executing drills in practice. Video is an excellent training tool. When you are able to see what has to be done, it's easier to replicate it. Similarly, if you are able to see what you are doing incorrectly, you'll find it easier to improve.

I have suggested to many players that they create a four- to five-minute highlight video of themselves playing at their best. A forward's video might show him on offense, skating well with speed and jump, taking a pass, going hard to the net, scoring, winning the puck on the boards, making good passes, and jumping into the play and going to the net. On defense, the video could show him working hard, being an aggressive checker, skating back, having good position, and covering his check.

Watching a positive performance video can strengthen the positive perception of your play and increase your confidence. It can also provide quality, high-performance images for your mental rehearsal. Remember, repetition builds strength, so watch your video often.

Some players have inserted clips of tigers and panthers on the hunt into their performance tape to create a stimulating video that puts them in a more competitive frame of mind. Others have added music. It can all work. Be creative. Developing players and veterans alike have found it beneficial to watch tapes of other players, both for pregame preparation and for viewing positive role models performing well.

Paul Kariya of the Anaheim Mighty Ducks told me he uses imagery more in conjunction with practice than for pregame preparation. He said he also uses video, especially to prepare against teams that he doesn't see very often. "We play Dallas and Los Angeles eight times a year. I know what to expect against them. I have found video to be especially helpful in preparing to play against the teams we meet once or twice a year to review their tendencies and weaknesses."

Some coaches use video as a motivational tool. Several teams I've worked with have made highlight tapes for big games and playoffs that feature some of the team's outstanding plays blended with music and crowd reactions. The idea is get players excited and positive about the challenge. It's an effective technique.

*Note:* Coaches who do this should be aware of the range of personality differences of their players. What lifts some players to their optimal arousal can sometimes get others too pumped up.

So far, I've mentioned that performance images should be positive. It's the same with video. However, viewing poor play can be useful for clarifying and eliminating mistakes. Once the mistakes are understood, though, you should focus on positive images.

Motivating highlight tapes usually emphasize a team's best plays, but in some cases, it can be beneficial to highlight the fallibility of the opposition. I recommended that idea to a coach in the playoffs when his team was facing an opponent who had dominated them all season. In such a case, it can be helpful and motivating to show the opposition's vulnerability. Highlight them making mistakes, being caught out of position, missing checks, getting knocked around and scored on, and allowing soft goals.

Similarly, facing an opponent with a hot goalie can cause some players to become uptight, negative, and discouraged. Video is one way to eliminate negative thinking such as "He can't be beaten." I once advised an NHL coach to prepare a tape showing Dominik Hasek, the goalie they were to face in the next playoff round, being scored on repeatedly.

*Note:* Always accompany these negative highlight tapes with a reminder that your success is about your *response-ability* to play winning hockey and not your opponent's tendency to break down.

When using video as a teaching aid, coaches need to remember that the desired behavior should be clearly defined. Roger Neilson is an expert at using the telestrator to show players exactly what he is looking for on the ice. "This gap is too big," he'll say. "This gap is just right. Keep your stick on him here. That's perfect. Take that angle away."

Coaches need to be clear about what they want to communicate with video. If players see what's desired, they can internalize the images into their mental rehearsal. Coaches shouldn't assume that everyone will appreciate what they have seen. One client, an NHL veteran, was given a game video by his coach and told in a critical manner to take it home and watch it. He did and couldn't find anything wrong with his play. As a matter of fact, he told me, "I didn't realize that I played so well. I don't know what the hell he's talking about."

Using video as punishment is not a wise strategy. One NHL coach who was angry with his team's disappointing performance in a game told the players to come in at 8:00 the next morning. When they arrived, he cued up the video of the previous night's game, said, "Watch this!" and stormed out of the room. One of the players told me how the team reacted: "It was real early. Half the team was dozing off, and hardly anyone really watched the tape." If anything, the exercise was a turn-off, not a turn-on. Indeed, it might have contributed to the players being less attentive viewers in the future.

Hockey is a game of emotions. You are scoring and winning—you feel good. You've been slashed—you get angry. You get beat—you become embarrassed. You miss the net—you get down on yourself. You're uncertain—you feel anxious. You're in control—you feel confident. As I said in chapter 1, success in hockey and in life is about learning how to manage your mind. It is difficult to manage your thoughts when your emotions are out of control (e.g., when you are angry, anxious, tired, or down). In the next chapter, we discuss the importance of creating right feelings, in particular, feelings of smoothness and power, and describe how to use breathing to help you do that.

Breathing is key. Breathing and releasing can help you relax, regain composure, and increase on-ice intelligence. Breathing and turning the wheel can help you energize, power up, and make things happen.

# HOMEWORK

## Assignment 1: Power Thoughts

Continue to work with your power words and affirmations. Select your six favorite power thoughts. Repeat them often.

## Assignment 2: Mental Rehearsal

In this chapter, I described three kinds of high-performance imagery to work with: mental rehearsal, imaging the successful end result, and stimulating imagery. For assignment 2, practice mental rehearsal. Sit back and relax. See yourself playing with confidence and ease. Visualize yourself handling the puck and skating well, with good eyes and making good reads. Run through your offensive and defensive ABCs.

## Assignment 3: Successful End Result

To create the image of a successful end result, choose a hockey goal you want to achieve. (Be sure you have an understanding of what you are striving for.) Hang a picture or drawing representing that image on your wall or someplace where you can see it. Solidify that image in your mind. Clarifying your intent is very empowering. Reflecting on that image can give you energy to carry on and can help you realize your goal or dream. Every so often, sit back and imagine yourself having achieved that goal.

## Assignment 4: Stimulating Imagery

Think of an animal with the qualities you want to bring to your game. Choose one that appeals to you and that you find stimulating. The big cats are especially popular because of their speed, balance, quickness, power, and beauty. Choose an image that works for you. Allow yourself to experience an awakening of your animal instincts. It can get your hockey juices flowing. Work hard and have fun.

## Assignment 5: Video

Study a video of one of your recent games. Look for things you do well and acknowledge yourself. Look for things you can improve and practice making that happen. From time to time, do a video review of your play.

If possible, make a two- to four-minute highlight video of yourself playing well both offensively and defensively.

# CHAPTER 4

# Controlling Emotions

Hockey is an intense, high-speed game. To play winning hockey, you must be able to manage your emotions and create right feelings. That means not only being able to energize, pump up, and attack, but also to calm down, regain composure, and play smoothly. Many players struggle with maintaining the right attack–smoothness balance. The exact balance point varies depending on a player's personality, experience, position, and role on the team.

The relationship between athletic performance and emotional arousal is depicted in figure 4.1. As emotional intensity increases (A), performance improves until it peaks (B). Thereafter, increases in intensity (overarousal) cause players to get too pumped or too tight and lead to a reduction in performance (C).

Being hockey tough is about managing feelings and focus so you can perform at your best. This is especially important in a high-speed, in-your-face, contact sport such as hockey. Under pressure, many players become tight, try too hard, force the play, squeeze the stick, chase the puck, retaliate, make mistakes, and compound errors. Others play flat and underaroused. They need to increase energy, intensity,

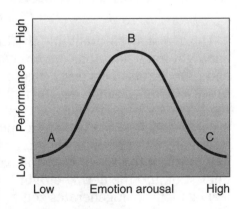

**Figure 4.1** Performance improves as emotional arousal increases but declines if emotional arousal is too high.

and often motivation to excel. The best and easiest way to control emotional arousal and create right feelings is to learn to use breathing effectively.

# EFFECTIVE BREATHING

Three things happen when you focus on your breathing. First, it unites your mind and body. Most performance problems are the result of the mind and body not performing as one. Thoughts and feelings are not in synch. It feels as though these two parts are operating at different speeds. Usually, the mind seems to be racing while the body lags behind. Focusing on breathing allows you to get it together and play more smoothly.

Second, breathing makes you focus on the present. When players feel anxious and worried, it's usually about the past (e.g., "How did I miss? Why didn't I shoot high when the goalie went down?") or the future (e.g., "What'll happen if I don't score or if I let in another soft one?"). They worry about mistakes made or mistakes to avoid. Worry lives in the past and future. Power is in the present. Focusing on breathing brings your consciousness (mind) into the here-and-now (present) world where the game of hockey is played. If you find yourself stuck worrying about the past or the future, take a breath and bring your attention back to the here and now.

**What helped me was working with my breathing, specifically, using my breathing to stay sharp and focused under pressure and then cool and calm when the pressure was relieved.**

*Glen Hanlon, former NHL all-star goalie, NHL coach*

Third, a smooth breathing rhythm can help you integrate left and right brain function. Our brains consist of two halves: the left and right cerebral cortexes (figure 4.2). The left half of the brain processes logical, analytic, and technical information. It helps you read the play and reminds you to play your position. It says, "Pick up your check, come back hard, play the body, be patient." The right half of the brain deals more with feeling and coordination. It allows you to gap up, take the pass, and deflect an 85-mile-an-hour shot into the net. The right brain is more spontaneous and feeling focused. It generates soft hands and the feeling of making the right moves.

Winning hockey requires smooth, integrated function between the left and right cerebral hemispheres, between feeling and focus. It's about knowing what to do and doing it. It's about the left brain thinking clearly, but not too much. It's about the right brain managing feelings and not letting strong emotions skew focus. Optimal performance occurs when the two halves of the brain perform in a coordinated and integrated fashion. Breathing smoothly is one of the simplest and most effective ways to facilitate that coordination and contribute to a high-performance state. Hockey toughness is about having focus, power, and emotional control. Breathing is a key to all three.

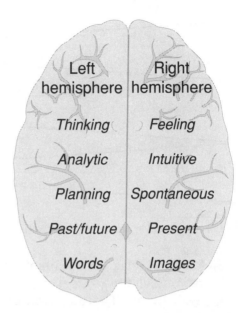

**Figure 4.2** The left and right hemispheres of the brain control different functions of thought and emotion. Breathing helps coordinate the functions of the left and right sides of the brain.

## Learning to Breathe

Here is a simple breathing process that is basic to emotional control and right feelings. It's one of the most important performance-enhancing techniques I use. Sit back. I'm going to ask you to experience three things in your breathing: rhythm, inspiration, and direction.

### Rhythm

The most important part of breathing is tuning into the rhythm of each breath (figure 4.3). By that I mean, as you breathe, simply feel the breath come in . . . and feel the breath go out.

Again, feel the breath come in . . . and feel it go out.

Spend a minute just experiencing your breathing. Feel the breath come in . . . and go out.

The key to rhythm is time. As you inhale, allow time for the in breath to come all the way in. As you exhale, allow time for the out breath to flow all the way out.

Breathing is like waves in the ocean. And waves never rush.

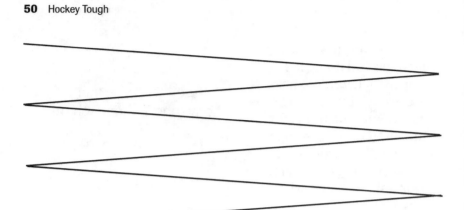

**Figure 4.3**   Feel the rhythm of your breath.

Sit back and relax. Give yourself time to feel each breath flowing in. Give yourself time to feel each breath flowing out.

It's very simple. There's power in simplicity.

### *Inspiration*

The second thing to focus on in breathing is the in-breath. If breathing is respiration, then the in-breath is the inspiration. To play winning hockey, you want to be inspired. To inspire yourself, tune into your breathing.

First, experience a smooth breathing rhythm. Now, as you breathe, place a little more emphasis on the in breath, on drawing in energy with each breath you take. Be aware that wherever you are, energy is all around you. Whether at home or on the road, whether before a game, between periods, or between shifts, with each breath you take you can draw in some of the energy around you. You have a personal connection to an unlimited supply of energy. Tap it. Remember, first experience a smooth breathing rhythm. Then draw in power.

### *Direction*

The third key to breathing is direction. Once you have experienced a smooth rhythm and can feel yourself breathing in energy, the next step is directing that energy. The direction can be internal or external. First, let's talk about directing energy internally to your hands, feet, and eyes.

Feel yourself breathing in energy. Then imagine sending energy out through your shoulders and arms and into the palms of your hands. Imagine that if you had a hockey stick in your hands, energy would flow right into the shaft of the stick and all the way down into the blade. Breathe smoothly and easily. On the in-breath, feel yourself breathing in energy. On the out-breath, imagine energy flowing down into your hands and into your stick.

Again, feel yourself breathing in energy. This time, direct the flow of energy down through your hips and quads, into your calves, and into the soles of your feet. Imagine that if you had skates on, the energy would flow into the blades of the skates.

Once again, experience a smooth, slow breathing rhythm. This time, as you breathe out, imagine you are sending energy up your spinal column into your head, and into your eyes. Imagine yourself seeing clearly. You can see the open man. Imagine you have great peripheral vision. You can read the play. You can anticipate and react.

## The Five-Pointed Star

The feeling image we are developing is like a five-pointed star. It involves sending energy out into the hands, feet, and eyes. Draw in energy and send it out through the arms and into the hands and stick, down through the legs and into the feet and skates, and up through the head and into the eyes like a five-pointed star (figure 4.4).

**Figure 4.4** Energy is sent through the arms and hands into the stick, through the legs and feet into the skates, and up through the head into the eyes.

Success in hockey requires good hands, good wheels, and good eyes. Whether you play forward, defense, or goal, feeling like a five-pointed star can help you excel. Pair feelings thoughts. As you breathe and direct your energy out, think or say to yourself, "I am a star."

Cliff Ronning is an inspirational player. He's a hockey tough little guy who for more than 16 seasons has weathered the hockey wars on six NHL teams while averaging close to a point a game. When I first met Cliff seven years ago, he impressed me as being a motivated, intelligent player who cared a great deal about doing well. Cliff was playing well, but in spite of his success, he worried about his performance, often running negative thoughts and focusing on past imperfections.

A couple of years ago, I asked Cliff, who was leading his team in scoring, how the work we did together has helped his game. I asked him how he used the training. Cliff said, "I use it all the time. I constantly go back over things you've said and written. I'm always tuning into my power thoughts and positive images of me playing well. I do it when things are going well and I do it when they're going badly. One of the things I've learned over the years is that there are always going to be ups and downs and it's not a good idea to be too focused on the result. Instead, focus on doing the right things. Focus on getting a good feeling in your hands, feet, and eyes, and doing your ABCs, and the good results will come."

Cliff says that good feelings are important to playing well. "Sometimes when I'm playing, I am able to create peace of mind. I think back to when I was a kid and I was just playing the game, loving the game and having fun. When I can create that feeling, there are none of the feelings of pressure to score and no worry about money. It's just working hard and having fun. That's when I play great."

He continued, "The breathing has really helped me. It's been huge. It's helped me to stay relaxed and to control my mind. It's amazing to realize how much control you can actually have of your mind and how you can tune out the stupid or negative thoughts and images and refocus on the basics that help you succeed."

Cliff also says that self-esteem is important. Remembering and visualizing times when you did things well builds confidence. "It's a constant battle at this level to play well. There are so many good players. You can't take anything for granted. It's really important to think about the basics and to work as hard as you can, physically and mentally. I think that the sport psychology training we've done has helped me to prepare better and focus on what's important and tune out the rest."

# RELEASING TENSION

Part of managing feelings has to do with being able to release feelings such as tension and negativity. Fear is the great limiter. Many players play with fear. Often it's fear of failure, of screwing up, making a mistake, letting the team down, or looking bad. Sometimes it's fear of injury. Fear causes tension and negativity. Tension is heavy. Hockey is a speed and reaction game, and tension can be a tiring and limiting drag.

Tension release is the channel-changing mechanism on your mental TV. Learning how to release tension and negativity is important to playing well. Sit back, relax, and breathe. Now experience the contrasting feelings of tension and release in five key body areas. (You might want to videotape yourself as you read this part and then practice with the tape as a guide.)

Let's start with the hands. Create some tension in your hands by making fists. As you do, feel the tension in the central part of the hand and the fingers. Now turn your wrists inward so you feel an additional tension in the back of your hands. Hold that position for four seconds. Feel the tension. Now let it go, and after you release it, take a breath. It's the action of releasing and breathing that allows you to clear the screen and change channels on your mental TV. This is the feeling you want to remember.

Our hands express our feelings. As I've said before, hockey players often squeeze the stick when they're trying too hard or when they're angry. The ideal is to play with strong arms and soft hands. By soft hands I mean a feeling in the palms of your hands that facilitates your passing, shooting, and stick-handling abilities.

Dick was a scrapper. He was also a player who sometimes tried too hard and therefore limited his touch around the net. Part of helping him handle the puck better was teaching him to release tightness and create soft feelings in his hands. At first, the image of soft hands didn't appeal to him. He thought of his hands as weapons. I explained that when I said "soft hands," I was talking about the palms of his hands. "The backs of your hands can be like steel," I told him, "but think of yourself with soft scorer's hands." He understood the distinction and used it to develop his puck-control skills.

The neck and shoulder area is where most athletes tense up when they're experiencing fear, whether it's fear of failure, embarrassment, or injury. It's a protective reflex, like a turtle pulling in its head when threatened. Although this response is protective, it is also limiting. It triggers a defensive "watch out" reaction rather than a more confident "go for it" attitude. Tightening in the neck and shoulders also interferes with breathing and reduces power and accuracy.

Raise your shoulders two to three inches. Hold that position for four seconds. Feel the tension. Now let go, release, and breathe. It's always release and breathe.

This time, raise your shoulders just half an inch. It's hardly noticeable, but you can feel the tension. Notice that as you tense, you cut down your breathing rate. Breath is power. Now release your shoulders, and after you do so, take a breath.

Billy had a good shot. In practice, when he was loose, he could shoot hard and with accuracy. But he wasn't nearly as smooth or effective in games. To be sure, he may have had less time to make a play in games than in practice, but while watching game video, we both could see that in game situations he just wasn't as smooth. "Yeah," he said. "I get tighter in games. I try too hard. I don't want to miss a chance. And the more I want to avoid making a mistake, the tighter I get and the more I miss." One way to help Billy was to remind him that any time he noticed tension in his neck and shoulders, he should release, breathe, and think "smooth."

Check your body for tension from time to time. If you notice tension in your neck, shoulders, or hands, remember to release and breathe.

As you practice relaxing and breathing, place one hand on your chest and the other on your abdomen. Feel these parts of your body expand and contract with each breath you take. I've compared breathing to the motion of waves in the ocean. Breathe easily and feel the waves rise and fall with each breath you take. Part of your pregame preparation or your postgame relaxation routines could include relaxed breathing with hands on the chest and abdomen.

The crotch or genital area is another tension-holding area. To create tension in the crotch, tighten the sphincter muscle as you would when holding back from going to the toilet. As you tighten the muscle, notice that your breathing is cut down. Hold the tension for four seconds, then release and take a breath. The point to remember is that you can tense or release any part of your body. You're the boss. You're in control. To generate right feelings, learn to scan the body for tension and let go of it. Holding tension anywhere reduces breathing, power, speed, and performance.

Last, curl your toes. Make fists with your feet, like a bird holding onto a perch. As you do, feel the tension in your feet. Hold for four seconds, then release and take a breath. Think about cats' feet; cats have great balance and acceleration.

Take a few relaxed breaths. As you do, feel yourself drawing in energy and sending it out to your hands, feet, and eyes. Feel energy flowing through you like a five-pointed star. Now scan your body. If any part of your body still feels tense, think of that part of your body as you release and breathe. Again, breathe in energy and allow it to flow through you. Allow yourself to feel powerful. Allow yourself to be a star.

The technique I've described is a simple, effective way to create feelings of smoothness and ease that will help you use energy effectively. The release reflex (figure 4.5) is key to mental management. It's the way to clear the screen on your mental TV. Release involves being aware, releasing, and breathing. You can use the release reflex to get rid of unnecessary tension and negative thoughts and to stay looser and have more emotional control. Remember, feelings affect thinking, and you're the boss. If you are feeling tense, angry, or frustrated, release, breathe, and clear the screen. Change your feeling and focus. Create a new, positive power thought. Be a star.

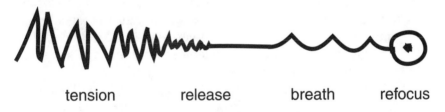

tension          release          breath          refocus

**Figure 4.5**   The release reflex clears the mental TV of negativity.

Now let's relate these feelings to hockey. Imagine that you are about to step onto the ice. Breathe smoothly and breathe in energy. Experience energy flowing through you like a five-pointed star.

Feel yourself sending energy out to your hands. Imagine having good hands, handling the puck well, making good passes tape to tape. Imagine quick, hard, accurate shots.

Feel yourself breathing in energy and sending it down to your legs. Imagine having good wheels. You feel strong on your skates and are skating with smoothness, speed, and power. You have good acceleration and jump.

Breathe in energy and send it to your eyes. Imagine that you see the ice clearly. You read the play well. You see the open man and the open space. You anticipate the play, angle your man to the outside, and take the puck away.

The definition of power is energy for work. A key to feeling more powerful is tuning into your breathing and drawing in energy, then directing that energy and allowing it to flow throughout your body.

Marg was a talented young center, a smart player who skated well, had good hands, and a good shot. However, like many hockey players, she would think too much and about too many things when she was under pressure. Often her thinking was negative, focusing on things she did wrong. This focus caused her to become tense, slowed her reactions, and reduced her touch. The more Marg struggled, the more she worried and the more tense she became. She worried that she wasn't scoring, that if she didn't produce she would get less ice time. The more Marg worried, the less productive she became and the less ice time she saw. It was a vicious cycle.

The first step in helping Marg turn her game around was to teach her to release and breathe, to create good feelings and a positive focus. Because Marg had an active mind and tended to worry, I showed her how to use that worry as a reminder to take a breath and focus on positive feelings and positive plays. Gradually, Marg became better able to change her feelings and manage her mind. As she did, her performance improved dramatically.

Breathing is key to managing your mind. It's key to filling yourself with energy and power. Power is a force that will work for you. Tap the mains. Draw in energy. Let energy flow through you. Be a star.

I consulted with Scott Gomez for a couple of years when he was playing junior hockey in the British Columbia and Western Hockey Leagues (BCHL and WHL). Scott is an intelligent player with great passion for the game. These qualities have contributed to him having a sensational NHL rookie season with the New Jersey Devils and being named the NHL rookie of the year.

When I asked Scott how the work we did helped his game, he replied, "One thing that I really got out of what we did together was the breathing. I use it all the time and in a lot of different ways. I use it the afternoon of a game to relax. Sometimes I get so excited about the game, I can't even take a nap. That's when I think of the waves and of breathing slowly and smoothly. It can really help me calm down. Sometimes I combine that breathing with imagining myself playing well."

Scott also uses breathing between shifts when he's on the bench. "I use my breathing both to calm down and to energize," he says. "If I notice I'm angry or frustrated, I take a breath. When I was play-

© Greg Forwerck/SportsChrome

Scott Gomez of the 2003 Stanley Cup champion New Jersey Devils uses effective breathing to keep himself calm and focused.

ing junior, I remember getting my ass kicked and snapping. And I remember you telling me to take a breath, stay cool, and focus on my ABCs. It all starts with that first breath: it helps you refocus and stay in control. It's important to be in control." Focus, aggression, and control are the keys to playing hockey tough.

Mark Hardy saw action as a defenseman in more than 900 games, most of them with the Los Angeles Kings, for whom he's now a coach. Mark told me, "When I was playing, the biggest thing for me was to be in control. I wanted to play with intensity, but I also wanted to have control. Control would allow me to go into the corner and be physical. It would help me stay calm and focused, make the right reads, and not chase the puck like a chicken with its head cut off. Breathing helped me to have control."

Like Scott Gomez, Mark used breathing to relax before combining it with visualization to get ready to play. He also used it on the bench to collect his thoughts and to stay in control during the game. "When I needed to, I used it to elevate my intensity," Mark says. "And I used it after the game to calm down and help me focus on the good things I did. Breathing is basic, and the training we did helped me for years."

It is very difficult to be both a good hockey player and the team's designated policeman. To be effective, you have to be in control to decide when to play and when to fight. I asked Ty Domi how he manages to play on the edge and yet maintain balance and control. He said, "You've got to have control. When things start to get away from you, you've got to take a few deep breaths and then refocus on all little things you've got to do."

Breathing is a way to calm down, regain composure, and play smooth, smarter hockey. It's also a way to energize, pump up, and attack. We've looked at smoothing. Now let's look at energizing and attacking.

## ENERGIZING

Hockey demands energy. Players use many ways to energize before a game. Some listen to music. Some exercise. Some take a cold shower. Some visualize themselves playing good hockey, and some talk positively or aggressively to themselves. But I feel that the most basic and powerful way to energize is to learn to use your breathing and turn the wheel.

Once again, focus on your breathing. This time, picture the breath as a wheel turning (figure 4.6). On the in-breath, the wheel turns up (A). On the out-breath, the wheel turns down (B). At this point, you are relatively relaxed so the wheel turns slowly. As you skate, your heart and respiratory rates increase and the wheel

**Figure 4.6** Breathing turns the wheel. The wheel turns up on the inhale (A) and down on the exhale (B).

turns faster and faster. Still, on the in-breath (inhale) the wheel turns up and on the out-breath (exhale) it turns down. Spend a minute or two experiencing your breath as a wheel turning.

*As the wheel turns, it generates power.* You are a power generator. It's a physical reality that as you breathe and turn the wheel, you generate power. As your heart beats and your lungs expand and contract, you pump blood, oxygen, and energy out through your body. You generate power. For a moment, experience yourself turning the wheel. Breathe in energy—feel the wheel turn up. Breathe out—feel the wheel turn down. Feel the wheel turn up, and draw in energy and power. Feel the wheel turn down, and send out the power.

Turning the wheel is a force that you can use to pump yourself up and direct your energy. It's important to direct energy out to the hands (good hands), to the feet (good wheels), and to the eyes (good eyes).

Winning hockey is about right feelings. It's about breathing in power and having good hands, good wheels, good eyes. It's about feeling like a star.

For good hands, pump up and turn the wheel. Breathe in energy and send it out into your hands. Imagine energy flowing right into the shaft and the blade of your stick. Imagine that feeling of having good hands and great stick control. Visualize yourself with great stick control.

For good wheels, turn the wheel again. Breathe in energy, and this time send it down through your hips and legs into the soles of your feet—cats' feet. Imagine skating well, feeling strong on your skates, having good balance and jump—having good wheels. Imagine skating with speed and power.

Finally, for good eyes, turn the wheel, draw in energy, and send it up to your eyes. Imagine that you can see clearly. You can see the open man and the open space. You can anticipate the play and react almost before things happen.

Now imagine being on the bench. Your shift is next. You want to be charged and ready. You remember to breathe, turn the wheel, draw in energy, and generate power. You send it into your hands and stick (good hands), down into your legs and feet (good wheels), and up into your eyes (good eyes). Imagine stepping onto the ice charged and focused. You're the boss. You control your feelings. If you notice that you are squeezing the stick or feeling too tight, then use your breathing and energy flow to create smooth feelings and be a star.

If you want energy to attack, turn the wheel. Whether you have been sitting on the bench the entire period or have been double-shifting and need a lift, breathe in energy, turn the wheel, and send power down to the drive train, through the arms into the hands, and up into the eyes. Then think positive and imagine yourself playing well.

Over the years, I have recommended this technique of turning the wheel and sending out energy to hundreds of hockey players. Here's how three NHL veterans used the technique.

Jamie was an experienced NHL defenseman who, after nine seasons in the league, had been relegated to a backup role. When I met him, he was getting about five minutes of ice time a game and only one or two shifts a period. He told me that even though he prepared himself well before the game, his energy level would drop after sitting for 10, 12, or 15 minutes, and it was hard for him to stay psyched and feel ready to go when called on. He asked if I could suggest a technique to help him feel more ready for those few minutes in each game when he would be asked to excel.

I showed Jamie how to use his breathing to turn the wheel and generate power while on the bench and how to send energy into his hands, feet, and eyes. I suggested that he do the exercise every five minutes, explaining that when he felt energized (like a star), he should watch the defenseman playing his position and imagine that he was on the ice, making all the right plays—playing the man, stepping up, making the pass, jumping up into the rush, and taking the shot.

Dan was an NHL veteran and all-star who got a great deal of ice time. After we had done some training, he confided being concerned that when he came off the ice after a hard shift, he had trouble keeping his mind on the game. I explained to him that it was quite normal for players coming off the ice to find it hard to concentrate on the game until they had caught their breath and regrouped.

This inability to concentrate is a good example of how feelings affect thinking. Exhaustion or oxygen debt is disorganizing. After a full, hard shift on the ice, a player needs to regroup for the next shift. The natural way to do that is simply to catch your breath. To do so, tune into your breathing rhythm. Once you can breathe smoothly and easily again, you'll be better able to concentrate effectively and focus on externals such as the play on the ice and getting your head back into the game. That whole refocusing process can take just a minute.

In his biography, NHL tough guy and all-star winger Dave "Tiger" Williams relates a story from the Canucks playoff run in the early 1980s that took them all the way to the Stanley Cup finals (Williams and Lawton 1984). As Tiger describes it, he was sitting on the bench during the third period. He was tired and his legs didn't feel good. "I needed to really bear down and produce some energy. I had to get the goddamned stuff from somewhere." He recalls that he thought of the things we had talked about, as well as his mother, who was always a source of energy for him. He describes asking for energy and taking a few breaths. As he says in the book, "When the game went into overtime, I got the energy and I got the winning goal."

Using breathing to energize is a good choice, but some players have made bad choices. Some professional hockey players have resorted to using stimulants to energize and get themselves up for a game. This isn't a good idea for a lot of reasons. Stimulants are unhealthy. They tax the body and can shorten a career . . . and a life. Psychologically, stimulants undermine confidence. A player using stimulants often becomes dependent and begins to think he needs something extra to play his game. Stimulants can also lead to inconsistent play. A player using stimulants may start out with a surge of energy but will sometimes run out of gas in the latter part of the game.

One NHL coach called me about a talented young player who developed a mental dependency on stimulants. He said, "He has really complicated his game and our game with this stuff he's taking. When he does use stimulants, sometimes he starts fine, but he's often low on energy in the third period when we really need him. The trainer tells me that sometimes they upset his stomach. And now when he doesn't take them he plays terribly. We're starting the playoffs and I don't want to change things dramatically, but at the end of the season I want him off the stuff. He has to find a better way to manage himself in the future."

Hockey tough is *not* about doing whatever it takes to perform. It's about learning healthy, effective ways to manage energy, focus, and emotion. It's also about developing a lifestyle that supports consistent high-level performance.

## ASSESS AND ADJUST

People are different. Some players need to calm down; others need to energize or pump up. An important strategy for success in hockey is to assess and become aware of who you are and what you need to do to perform your best. Try to find an approach to right feelings that might be beneficial to you, and discover when and how you can best implement it.

Try combining breathing with power words, as discussed in chapter 2. The specific word you choose depends on who you are and what you want. If you find yourself pushing too hard or playing too tight, take a breath and think "smooth." On the other hand, if you want to generate the energy to forecheck more aggressively, win the boards, go hard to the net, or come back and shut down your check, turn the wheel and think "attack." Thinking "attack" works whether you are on offense or defense. Off the ice, if you want to generate power for a workout in the gym, you can also turn the wheel and think "attack."

Larry was very skeptical about breathing exercises. "I just don't see how taking a few breaths is going to help me play better hockey," he told me. Later he confided that he thought the whole sport psychology idea was useless. Then one day he tried using breathing for his workouts in the gym. He suddenly realized how much more power he could generate if he focused on his breathing. After that experience, it made sense to bring that skill and power with him onto the ice. He started to use his breathing and the thought of attacking in his battles along the boards and whenever he drove to the net.

Hugo was a talented junior player and a professional prospect. Although he was motivated to play well, he came to see me because, as he put it, "I'm in a slump." When I asked him what he meant, he replied, "Something weird is happening to me. I don't feel good on the ice, and I'm not scoring any goals." I asked him to be specific about what did not feel good on the ice. He replied that normally he was a very good skater but was feeling slow. He also felt he didn't have good touch around the net. To check for health issues, I asked Hugo how he felt away from the ice. He said he felt fine. He was sleeping and eating normally. "It's just that I don't feel as fast or as sharp," he said "and I've been missing the chances I've been getting."

"What does it feel like when you're playing great?" I asked him.

Without hesitating, he replied, "I feel quick, confident, and sharp. And I put the puck in the net."

"Do you think that maybe you're pressing or trying too hard?"

"Yeah, I probably am," said Hugo. "I've got to get drafted this year."

I asked him to tell me about a time when he was playing great hockey. He thought for a moment, then answered, "Last year in the playoffs I scored eight goals. And this year I played well at the start of the season."

"Tell me again," I asked, "what does it feel like when you're playing well?"

"I told you," he replied. "I feel fast and sharp and confident."

It was time to pose an important question. "Instead of having to play great and score goals to feel good, what if you were to create those good feelings first. Do you think you would play better and score more?"

"Yeah, I probably would," he said. "Yeah, sure."

"Then why," I asked, "do you create the other tense, slow feelings?"

"I'm not doing it on purpose," Hugo protested.

"But you are doing it, Hugo. You're the boss." Then I asked, "If I were to show you or remind you how to feel good on the ice, would that help?"

"Sure it would," he said, and he asked me to show him how to feel good.

Now that I had Hugo's full attention, I explained to him how the mind works, how tension can create negative feelings and negative thoughts, which in turn create more negative feelings. And how tension makes people feel slow, tight, and tired. That rang a bell for Hugo. "Yeah," he said. "I've been feeling really tired at the end of my shifts."

Over the next two sessions, I showed him how to use his breathing to create more ease and power and how to get that power flowing out to the points of the star. I told him that whenever he felt tense or tired, he should take a breath, turn the wheel, generate power, and send energy out to his hands, feet, and eyes. "The game is hands, feet, eyes," I told him.

Hugo followed my advice. He practiced breathing daily on and off the ice. He imagined himself smooth, light, and fast, making all his good moves. Before long, Hugo was playing like Hugo again.

# HOMEWORK

## Assignment 1: Breathing Recap

Work with your breathing. (Refer back to Learning to Breathe, The Five-Pointed Star, and Releasing Tension.) Create a 10-minute breathing routine to use every day. Sit or lie back, get into your breathing, experience a smooth breathing rhythm, one in which the waves flow in and the waves flow out. As you experience rhythm, emphasize the in breath and drawing in energy, then feel that energy flowing out through the body like a five-pointed star.

## Assignment 2: Breathing, Affirmations, and Imagery

Combine breathing with affirmations and imagery. After about five minutes of relaxed breathing, spend a couple of minutes imagining yourself on the ice, skating with smoothness, power, and ease. If you are a forward or defenseman, imagine handling the puck well, making good passes, having good touch and a hard accurate shot. Imagine playing good defense, playing the man and finishing your checks. If you are a goalie, imagine having good position and angles, being square to the shooter, seeing and stopping each shot, and moving well in the net.

Run through your affirmations. After each one, remember to take a breath and visualize yourself as the player in your mental image.

## Assignment 3: Ice Application

On the ice, experience yourself breathing in energy. Feel energy flowing through you. When you come off the ice at the end of a shift, pick up your breathing for 8 to 10 breaths. Just watch the breath flow in and out to the hands, the feet, and the eyes. Breathe and send energy out like a five-pointed star.

## Assignment 4: Breathe and Stretch

As you stretch before a game or practice, remember to release and breathe. Combining breathing with stretching can give your muscles more oxygen, more energy, and a better stretch.

## Assignment 5: Attack or Smooth

Determine whether you are someone who would benefit more by attacking or by smoothing. Begin to practice shifting gears and powering up or down by using breathing.

# CHAPTER 5

# Winning Hockey Attitude

A winning attitude is a way of thinking that predisposes you to being more successful. With a winning attitude, almost anything is possible. Being hockey tough means having a winning attitude, and attitude is a matter of choice.

During a meeting with a championship-caliber junior hockey team, I asked the players, "What contributes to a winning attitude?" One player answered, "Being positive." When I asked him to be more specific, he said, "Thinking positive thoughts. Knowing what you want to do and thinking you can do it." We had been working with imagery, so another player added, "It's having positive images, like seeing yourself playing well and saying positive things to yourself." "What else?" I asked the group. The answers came fast:

"A winning attitude is about being motivated."

"It's working hard for what you want."

"Confidence is part of a winning attitude."

"So is pride."

"Mental toughness."

"Expectation."

"Self-esteem."

"You're all right," I chimed in. "Many qualities make up a winning attitude." Let's spend a few minutes talking about what we can do to strengthen some of these winning qualities.

# COMMITMENT

Success begins with motivation. Motivation is what moves us to action. It's about desire, goals, and commitment. As I said at the outset of the book, goals work. Setting goals clarifies direction and increases success. But setting goals and repeating your goal statement aren't enough; you have to do the work. Some players set excellent goals for themselves but are simply not willing to follow through with the day-to-day action necessary to make their goals a reality. Commitment is the willingness to do what's necessary to get the result you want.

Your commitment is a reflection of your motivation. If your goal is to get to the top of the mountain, the way up is one step at a time, rain or shine. Taking the time, spending the energy, and making it happen are what commitment is all about. In hockey, one step at a time means doing the day-to-day physical and mental training needed to build up the fitness base, skill sets, productive focus, emotional control, and positive attitude required to excel. It's making yourself more *response-able* and hockey tough.

Consistent hard work is an expression of commitment and it's essential to success. When I asked Pavel Bure what advice he had for a young player wanting to develop his scoring ability, he said, "The only advice I have is general. Work hard."

Similarly, Wayne Gretzky, the perennial NHL all-star and Hall of Famer, was quoted as saying, "I'm gifted, but I've worked hard for everything I've gotten. Gordie Howe and Bobby Orr worked hard too. Like them, I didn't say, 'I'm gifted. I don't have to work hard anymore'" (Ferguson 1990).

Commitment is the willingness to put in the necessary time and effort to excel. Willingness means making a choice. From a mental training standpoint, it goes back to a principle we discussed in chapter 1: Whatever comes up, *use it*. Either you use it or it will use you. If you are genuinely committed to being the best you can be, then it's important to learn how to use it, whatever situation, challenge, or obstacle is confronting you.

The process of using it involves clearing the screen on your mental TV and refocusing on the positive. When people perceive a challenging stimulus, their initial response is often automatic. Using it is about activating the release reflex: releasing (tension, negativity, or anxiety), breathing in energy and power, and refocusing on the positive—what you want to do on the ice, your ABCs, being a star, being a scorer, being a winner, or being a tiger.

Cliff had been centering a line that had scored almost a hundred goals during the NHL season. Just before the playoffs, he was switched to a line with two hard-working checkers as his wingers. At first, he was upset with the line change. He saw himself as a scorer and setup man, and he wondered, "How can I play with these guys?" Obviously, he had no control over the line change. What he could control was his reaction to it. I asked him, "How can you use it?" When he didn't respond, I said, "You've been seen as a one-dimensional player, an offensive guy. Here's an opportunity to develop your complete game. This new line can become an excellent checking line, and when life gives you lemons, it's best to make lemonade." He accepted the challenge, changed his focus, and used it to become a more complete player. All the way to the Stanley Cup finals, he played winning hockey, and the line he centered was acknowledged as the team's best line throughout the playoffs.

Winners are not free from disappointment, fear, and negativity. Like everyone else, they experience uncertainty and doubt. It's just that they don't dwell on it. Instead, they use it to refocus and stay on the power channel. Winners use everything.

On a visit to Sault Ste. Marie, Ontario, in 1995, I met with Harry Wolfe. Harry was the voice of the Soo Greyhounds for more than four decades. Harry pointed out two NHL prospects playing with the Greyhounds, explaining that both had been at NHL training camps and both had been sent back to the junior team. There was a huge difference between the two, however.

One of the players was sulking about the decision to return him to his junior team. He thought he shouldn't have been sent down, that they hadn't given him a fair chance. Since returning to his team, he had been negative, full of complaints, and was playing poorly.

The other player had a completely different spin on his experience at the NHL camp. He said, "What I realized is that I can play up there. I'm good enough. It was great, and I'm going back." Since being sent back to junior, he was working hard and playing very well. Which of the two players do you think made it back? If you chose the second one, you're right. The second player used his experience. The first one let it use him. Remember, attitude is a matter of choice, and winners use everything.

Being hockey tough is learning how to use it. Whether you are a player or a coach, set a standard of commitment for yourself and model it for your teammates or colleagues. Become more aware of what's happening around you, and whatever presents itself, choose to use it.

I've spoken with many parents about their sons' and daughters' development as hockey players. One dad gave his 16-year-old son, an NHL prospect, some sound advice when the young man left home to play in the Western Hockey League. He told his son that most of the players on the team were not going to go any further than junior hockey. He said, "If you're motivated and committed to going beyond that level, then don't just be one of the guys. Involve yourself and emulate the work habits of the players on your team who are winners, who share a motivation and commitment to develop their abilities, to go further and be the best they can be."

That's good advice. Scotty Bowman said the same thing when I asked him about commitment and developing potential. He said, "If you want to improve at something, anything, get involved with people or players who are better than you. Then you'll get better."

Hockey is a team game. Even though you may be focused and trying to avoid hassles, it's not always easy to get along with all teammates and coaches. Take Karen, for example, a dedicated 16-year-old player. We had been discussing her goals and her commitment when she complained about a self-centered teammate who was making her life miserable. "She really bugs me," Karen said. "She's selfish. All she thinks about is herself, on and off the ice. I know I have to get along with her. Do you have any suggestions?"

I suggested to Karen that this player was giving her a refocusing opportunity, and if she was really committed to being the best, she could and should use the situation rather than allow it to use her. "How do I do that?" she queried.

"First, I would try talking to her," I replied.

"Impossible," she said. "I've tried half a dozen times. She's a jerk."

"Then I suggest that every time you notice her behaving like a jerk, you take a breath, clear your stress off the screen. Instead of getting upset, see yourself making a pass, putting the puck in the net, or checking your opponent out of the play. Remind yourself, 'I'm focused and nothing can get me off track.' If she bugs you 10 times during a practice, that's an opportunity to do 10 positive reps (e.g., 10 passes, 10 goals) of yourself playing well."

Adapting something Goethe, the great writer and philosopher, is alleged to have said, I say, "If it doesn't kill you, use it to make you stronger."

## Define Your Commitment

Review your hockey goals. What are your long- and short-term goals, both for you individually and for your team? What's your commitment? What price are you willing to pay to achieve your goals? Now choose one thing about your game that has been using you and getting you down and think of how you can use it to be a more effective player.

# CONFIDENCE

Confidence is another key to a winning attitude. Confidence has to do with how we see ourselves. A person who is confident believes he or she can do the job. That belief makes it more likely the job will get done. Two important questions for most athletes are "How do I increase confidence?" and "How do I transform doubt and negativity into the confident sense of being a winner?"

I think there are two basic ways to build confidence. Late one evening I got a phone call from an NHL coach who was aboard the team plane heading home after a disappointing loss. The team had been losing consistently, and this particular defeat was just too much. The coach wanted me to speak to his players the next day about confidence.

When I entered the room, the players were all assembled. After being introduced, I began by asking, "What builds confidence?" The room was silent. Finally, one player, the captain, said, "Winning." He was right, of course. The most basic way to build confidence is to experience success. Success leads to more success. Success in the form of winning and scoring builds confidence. However, confidence is fragile. If you are a scorer and you haven't been scoring, you can begin to feel anxious and self-doubt can creep into your thinking. Scoring erases the self-doubt. If a team has been losing repeatedly and blowing leads, their thinking can become negative; they will begin to anticipate failure—"Oh no, it's happening again" or "There's no way"—and their confidence will disappear. After a win or two, players begin to think more positively and more confidently.

**It's not the size of the dog in the fight that matters as much as the size of the fight in the dog.**

*Don Cherry, former NHL coach and hockey commentator*

Martin Lapointe, NHL winger, said, "When you are not scoring, I think your confidence is getting lower and lower, game after game. It's always behind your mind. You try not to think about it, but obviously it's in your mind. You squeeze the stick a little harder. It's like a snowball effect. Even though you don't want to think about it, it's just there."*

Markus Naslund, an NHL all-star winger and captain of the Vancouver Canucks, made another interesting comment about scoring and confidence. Markus told me, "When I am playing well and scoring goals, I look forward to every shift. I think positive. I think and feel like I can score every time I get on the ice. When I haven't scored in several games, I notice that I start thinking more negatively. Thoughts like 'How long will this scoring drought last?' start creeping into my mind." These thoughts vanish quickly after he scores a goal or two.

The experience Markus describes is common. After performing well, people feel more confident, and that has a positive influence on their play. The trick is to learn to create those confident feelings before the result to increase the probability of the result happening.

John was a scorer. He had been a scorer and an all-star in junior hockey and had led his team to a national championship. That success carried over when he began his pro career. But one day John telephoned and said, "I'm in a slump. Since the all-star game (two weeks before), I haven't been able to score and my confidence is gone." He asked me if I could help him regain his confidence and his scoring touch.

I listened to him, took a breath, and replied, "John, you're a scorer. Scorers sometimes have periods when they score less. If you're worried about it, I'll recommend a few things you can do to start scoring again. The first thing is to remember to relax and breathe."

"I'm doing that," he replied. "I do it in the afternoon before a game. And I focus on my breathing when I'm waiting to go on the ice, just before the start of each period."

"Good," I replied. "The second thing is mental rehearsal. It's helpful to visualize scoring goals like you can, in every possible way. Imagine working hard, going hard to the net, and scoring. Imagine yourself one-timing a pass and scoring. Imagine scoring from the

---

*Martin Lapointe quote reported on ESPN.com, February 10, 2003.

slot. Imagine jumping on a rebound and popping it in. Imagine scoring on a good shot. Imagine scoring top corner, bottom corner, and five-hole. Imagine deflecting a shot into the goal. Imagine someone banking one in off your back or your bottom into the net. Imagine yourself scoring goals and having fun. I want you to score 50 imaginary goals twice a day. Do you know what I mean?"

John said he knew what I meant and that he would do some positive imagery. "Remember," I added, "every time you have a negative or worrisome thought, take a breath and imagine scoring a goal."

The third thing I told John to do to sharpen his goal-scoring reflex was to practice. "Practice moving the puck with your linemates. Practice your shot. Practice one-timing a pass. Practice tip-ins. Practice does make perfect," I reminded him.

"The fourth thing to remember, John—and it's important to know this in your bones and say it to yourself again and again—is that you are a good hockey player. You are good at generating chances and putting the puck in the net. You are a scorer. That's who you are. You love to play hockey. You love to work hard. You love to score goals. Follow this advice, John, and the goals will happen." When I spoke to him a week later, the drought was over and he was scoring again.

The number-one answer to the question of what builds confidence is success. Success, winning, scoring, and shutting down the opposition all lead to confidence. But what if you haven't had success lately or at this level? What can you do to grow your confidence when you haven't been winning or scoring? The answer lies in preparation.

If you look up from the valley at a high mountain peak, the task of climbing the mountain may seem overwhelming. You may lack the confidence and belief that you can do it. However, the task becomes less daunting if you break down the climb into steps and stages, with many steps constituting a stage. If you know from your training that you can take these steps and complete each stage, your confidence that you can complete the climb will grow.

In climbing your hockey mountain, visualize yourself taking the steps necessary to build your strength, skills, fitness, and ability to read the game. Approach your development in steps and stages. Break down the challenge into manageable steps and do what's necessary.

Regaining confidence and returning to top form following an injury requires the same approach. Set your goal and some attainable intermediate goals. See yourself doing the basics and performing well at each stage. As you do, your belief in your ability will grow. You'll know that you can do it. Just as I advised John, use mental rehearsal to visualize yourself doing it, then actually do it in practice. Finally, make or allow it to happen in game situations. Two affirmations that are relevant and worth repeating are "My mind is a force I use to make things happen" and "Self-love is allowing myself to win."

Corey was an outstanding college player and an all-star defenseman in the American Hockey League. He had several NHL call-ups but never seemed to stick very long. When I met him, he was playing great in the AHL. He was both a defensive and offensive force for his team and a go-to guy on the power play.

As we spoke, Corey mentioned how much he wanted another shot in the NHL. Shortly after our meeting, he was given that opportunity, and I watched him in his first few games back in the NHL. Initially, he was tentative, cautious, and appeared overly conservative. I told him so. Corey explained that he was very confident in the minors, where he had the green light from the coach to take chances, rush, shoot the puck, attack back door, whatever he thought would work. But at the NHL level, he was afraid of making a mistake.

I told Corey that his confident play in the minors was the reason the big-league club had called him up—he was the guy who could make the plays. "While I understand your concern about making a mistake," I told him, "if you play a tentative, 'watch out' game, you're not showing them who you can be, and you may not be around very long."

Corey appreciated the feedback. It reminded him to be himself. I encouraged him to build his confidence by using his anxiety to visualize himself as the take-charge guy he was capable of being and to play that way. As he became more aggressive, he had more impact and more fun.

Playing good defense is a daunting task. However, as you break down the challenge into various elements, what has to be done becomes clearer and seems more possible. To excel on defense is a matter of developing skating skill and the ability to read the game, maintain good position, play strong without the puck, clear the front of the net, play against size, handle the puck, play against speed, gap up, get the puck out of your end, pass on the tape, control the puck at the point, and shoot from the point. To build confidence, mentally rehearse each of these elements, then practice them on the ice until you feel "I can handle this." Then move on to another challenging part of your game. Work consistently with focus, feeling, and commitment until gradually you develop the sense that "I can do it."

Practice the things you have to work on to become a better player. Practice on the ice. Practice in practice. Practice with mental rehearsal. Practice until you know you can do it, until you can honestly tell yourself, "I am strong on my skates. My skating continues to improve. I read the play well. I gap up. I play the body. I always have good position. I keep my man to the outside. I pin him on the boards. I take his stick away. I clear the front of the net. I get the puck out of our end. I make the good outlet pass. I jump into the play. I am comfortable and effective at the point. I make good reads and good passes. I shoot hard and with accuracy. I am in control." As you practice these elements and see your ability improve in each area, your performance and self-image as a competent defenseman will improve and your confidence will grow.

Chain together the elements in your mental rehearsal. For example, visualize yourself breaking up a play in your end, handling the puck with composure, making the good outlet pass, and jumping up into the play. With practice, your confidence as a playmaker and defender will grow.

**Before every game, I would picture guys coming down the ice and I knew I could stop them.**

*Mark Hardy, LA Kings coach and veteran defenseman*

In chapter 2, I described how Luke, an NHL winger, used his ABCs, breathing, and imagery to improve his power-play performance. Years later, when I discussed the experience with Luke, he said, "What we did really helped me rebuild my confidence. You helped me structure a plan and get my mind uncluttered and refocused on executing that plan. I had all this other negative stuff in my head, and I was starting to worry and lose hope. I knew I could do it, but the question was, how? You helped me unravel the clutter and put together a how-to plan so my energies could go into doing it, instead of being confused about what to do. Once I got past that, I started to believe, 'Yes, I can,' and then I began to play better."

## Design Your Own Confidence-Building Training Program

Assess and adjust. Identify some parts of your game that challenge you, where you feel your confidence is limited. Think about what elements you have to improve to perform more effectively. Think about what you have to do to really master these elements. What on-ice practice would improve your confidence in these areas? What self-talk and imagery would help? Act on your commitment and do the practice. Preparation builds confidence. See yourself practicing and improving.

The easiest answer to the question "How do I build my confidence?" is simply "Improve your preparation and change your focus." Magic happens when you set small incremental goals. Make a commitment, work consistently, run positive programs, mentally rehearse, think power thoughts, keep moving forward, take steps, complete stages, say positive things to yourself, and acknowledge yourself for improving on each element or stage. Use unsuccessful experiences to improve your play. Use successful experiences to increase your confidence. Then move on to the next element. Chain the elements together. Run positive programs, positive self-talk, and positive imagery on your mental TV.

Nobody is perfect. Remember that when you experience a poor shift—if you play defense and you get caught out of position and get beat, if you are a scorer and you miss the open net, if you are a goalie and you allow a soft goal—use it. Use your mistakes to your advantage. Think of what you can do to improve your performance next time. Frame your efforts in a positive light. As you do, your performance will improve and your confidence will grow.

I spent several years consulting in the National Football League. One of the high-pressure jobs in football is field-goal kicker. From a pressure standpoint, it's a little like being a goalie. A kicker's performance can be affected by confidence. A regular routine the Rams kicker went though at each practice to build his confidence was to start by kicking short field goals, or chip shots, from the 10-yard line. After making two or three kicks in a row, he would move to the 15-yard line. With success at each distance, he'd move back farther—to the 20-, 25-, 30-yard line, and so on. As he progressed though this regular practice routine, he strengthened his confidence as well as his perception of himself as a competent kicker.

The point I want to reiterate, based on what I've observed in every sport, is that confidence flows from preparation and success. Do the work necessary to experience success in the elements and steps to your ultimate goal, and your confidence will grow. Building success and confidence is directly related to improving the quality of mental preparation.

# SENSE OF DESERVING

Another expression of a confident, winning hockey attitude is what I call a sense of deserving or expectation. Confronted with a goal-scoring opportunity, some players just go for it. It's as if they feel they deserve it and they're going to take it. Most scorers have this quality. They expect the pass or chance to be there, and they don't hesitate to shoot the puck. Others don't feel as confident. It's as though they don't expect success or they need permission to go for it. Sometimes you get the sense that they think too much.

A sense of deserving is a matter of attitude. It's believing you deserve to exhibit your ability. The opportunity is here for me and it's mine. There's no holding back. Remember, if you don't believe you deserve it, it's unlikely you're going to make it happen. A method I have found useful in helping athletes who don't feel deserving or confident about their ability in a particular situation is to have them go back to feeling deeply relaxed and powerful and build step-by-step from there.

## Learn to Feel Deserving

If feeling undeserving is an issue for you, here's a three-step process you might use to increase your sense of deserving.

First, sit back and tune into your breathing rhythm. Allow time for each breath to come all the way in and go all the way out. Relax. Breathe slowly and smoothly. As you do, remind yourself that you deserve your time. I'm not just talking about understanding the idea, but about actually experiencing a feeling. As you begin to experience the benefits of allowing enough time in your breathing rhythm, acknowledge that you deserve your time.

Now imagine being on the ice. Imagine skating well with ease, speed, and power. As you do, affirm that you deserve to exhibit your ability, all your ability. Know and feel that you deserve to exhibit your ability.

Finally, bring that awareness and sense of deserving to a game situation. If you find yourself in a game with more experienced players or up against a team that has outplayed you in the past and start to feel less powerful and less confident, then use this *dis-ease* to go deeper into your breathing and acknowledge what you know to be true, "I deserve to exhibit my ability." Then bring that sense of deserving into the game. Something I often say to young players to remind them of their sense of deserving is "It's your puck. Play like it's your puck."

# IDENTITY

Identity is another ingredient in a winning attitude. Your identity is who you think and feel you are, and to a lesser extent, it's who others perceive you to be. For most of us, our identity evolves with time and life experience. Most successful players have some identity or image of themselves as effective competitors. Your hockey identity can determine how you behave and perform as a player. Most important, it's something you can shape and control. As I've said before, you get more of what you think about. If you think you can, you may. If you think you can't, you won't. *The way you talk to yourself and visualize yourself performing are two important determinants of your identity or self-image.* Your hockey identity can give you the energy and confidence that will lift you to excel, or it can act like a weight to slow you down, tire you, and keep you from reaching your potential.

Doug Risebrough, the general manager of the Minnesota Wild, told me a story from his playing days with the Montreal Canadiens. At that time, the Canadiens, a perennial NHL powerhouse, were playing an expansion team, one to which they had never lost a game in the Montreal Forum. At the end of the second period, the Canadiens were behind by three goals. In the dressing room, surrounded by mementos of past Canadiens championship teams, the players were obviously angry with their on-ice performance (or lack of it). Doug says the mood among the Canadiens players was "That's not who we are to lose to these bums." And the Canadiens stormed back onto the ice and scored three goals in the third period.

I had a call from an AHL coach whose team had won their division in the regular season but were beaten decisively by a sixth-place team in the first game of the playoffs. "We played poorly," the coach said. He was concerned and asked for a suggestion on how to refocus the team.

I asked him what he meant when he said the team had played poorly. Exactly what did the players do in the previous night's game that was different from what they had been doing all year long? "We were tight," he replied. "We were forcing everything. We didn't play smart. We were too aggressive. We didn't stay high on the forecheck. We pinched and got caught. And we chased the puck." He had a theory as to why the team had reacted that way and wondered if it was a good idea to discuss it with the players.

"Keep it simple," I told him. "Focus on their identity; remind them who they are. Show them some video clips of last night's poor performance and say, 'That's not acceptable, and that's not who we are.' Encourage them to play smart, to remember their ABCs. Then show them some video highlights from the season in which they played exemplary hockey and tell them, 'That's who we are. All year long we prided ourselves on being smart and working hard. That's who we are. If we play like that, we'll win.'"

Scotty Bowman says that a team's identity is one of the most important ingredients in winning. I agree. An identity image of who you are and how you can and should perform can move you to do things that you think yourself physically incapable of doing. The same is true of a team. Conversely, wearing the identity or self-image of a loser or a choker can be limiting. Our identity can lift us to superior performances, or it can slow us down and limit us.

Identity is not a static entity. Identity is something that has been formed over time and by experience, and it can be reshaped. You can change your identity by changing your mind. The word *repent* comes from the French word *penser*, "to think." To repent means to think again. We tend to associate repentance with a particular kind of mind change, with making a commitment to stop sinning. Well, when you think negative things about yourself, you create a loser's identity, and that is a form of sinning. It's limiting, and it's a signal that it's time to rethink. Change your mind. Becoming hockey tough means creating a positive self-image. Remember, you're the boss, and attitude is a matter of choice.

In chapter 2, I discussed affirmations and power statements. These are identity statements. You can use them to define and strengthen your identity. As I said before, your affirmations and power statement should represent who you are and what you aspire to be. Your identity should be a mix of truths and affirmations.

## Create an Identity Statement

Prepare your own personal identity statement. Write a statement of who you are (or could be) at your best. Affirm all your strengths and highlight your potential. If you haven't yet manifested a desired quality, incorporate it into your identity statement. Read this statement to yourself and repeat it often. Let it become you.

Psychologists who do ability testing know that the absence of a high score doesn't necessarily mean a lack of ability. It simply means the person being tested didn't perform well on that day. When you have a poor shift or a poor game, don't latch onto that disappointing perception and keep rerunning it as an identity program of who you are. Instead, use it. Say to yourself, "That's not who I am." Then imagine skating with speed and power and performing well. Remember, to improve your performance identity (and increase your confidence), think about and visualize yourself at your best, then work toward making it a reality.

For too many athletes, their sense of well-being is determined by how they perform. If they do well, they feel good about themselves. If they perform poorly, they feel terrible or worthless. It's normal for people who are highly motivated and who work very hard to achieve certain performance goals to be disappointed with poor performance. However, it's important to stay positively focused on your commitment. Remember and affirm that you are on a positive track and that nothing can take you off that track. If you have a good practice or game, acknowledge yourself. Rerun your highlight reel, either on video or with mental rehearsal imagery. Repeat your affirmations and power thoughts. If you have a poor shift, practice, or game, don't let that shake your confidence. Instead, say, "That's not who I am," and then see yourself making the plays.

I asked Pavel Bure how he deals with the close checking and clutch-and-grab tactics in today's game of hockey and what he says to himself during the game to keep himself positively focused. Pavel's answer contained some good advice, especially for those who tend to overreact to their performance on each and every shift. He said, "The two things I say to myself are 'Don't get frustrated' and 'Just keep working hard.'"

# PRIDE

*Pride*—most players have heard the word and most coaches have used it to rally their players. I asked a 14-year-old bantam player, "What does pride mean to you?" Without a moment's hesitation, she replied, "It's feeling good about what I do and what my team does."

Pride is a composite of many qualities of a winning attitude. It's related to motivation, commitment, confidence, identity, and self-esteem. Pride is having a positive sense of who you are, how you choose to represent yourself, and what you have done. In hockey, pride is related to self as well as to team. If your identity is that of someone motivated and committed to being the best you can be, then it follows that you take pride in performing well. Playing well requires preparation, so you would also take pride in preparing to be at your best.

Pride in your team means that you identify with or tie your self-image to the team's performance. It means you commit to and derive satisfaction from the team playing well. When a team is successful, the confidence and pride of its players increase. However, pride isn't exactly the same as winning. It's about doing your best. That often means success.

How do you build a sense of pride? I turned to an expert, Mark Messier, who for more than 20 years has been the embodiment of pride and a winning attitude. I asked Mark how he would encourage a young player to develop pride. He replied that there is no simple answer. So many things go into developing a sense of pride, he said, including the way a child is brought up, its values, work ethic, and self-esteem. And people are different. What inspires some people is completely different from what motivates and drives others. Some people feel proud when they win. Others win and feel disappointed.

Mark went on to say that Canadians think of themselves as living in the best hockey nation in the world. They take pride in how they play the game. If a player is selected to put on a Team Canada jersey, a real sense of pride goes with that. That sense of pride moves you to want to play and to be as good as you can be because of what it stands for and because of who you are. "If I'd have to pin it down,"

© Craig Melvin/Sportschrome

Mark Messier has exemplified pride and attitude for more than two decades in the NHL.

Mark concluded, "I guess pride is about being your best. It's meeting your expectations and those of others. But most important, it's meeting the expectations you set for yourself."

## Eight Steps to Building Pride

1. Relax and breathe. Begin to think about and imagine yourself playing to the best of your ability, really playing well. Visualize the good stuff.

2. Run through your ABCs. See yourself making all the plays. Acknowledge that image. Say, "That's who I am." Take on that identity of you at your best.

3. Make the commitment to be the best you can be.

4. Do the work to make it happen—in the weight room, on the bike, on the ice, at practice. Combine that with mental training.

5. Be consistent. Work at it every day. Give 100 percent every game and every shift.

6. Evaluate your progress. Find something positive to acknowledge, even if it's just your dedication and work ethic. Find some area that needs more attention and improve on it.

7. Walk your talk. Model your commitment and determination to your teammates.

8. As you put your heart and soul into it, slowly but surely your sense of pride in who you are, what you are trying to accomplish, and what you are able to do will grow every day.

## LOVE THE GAME

Last but not least, *love* the game. In describing a hockey tough mind-set, we talked about power programs, the thoughts, images, and attitudes that you can use to generate the energy, emotion, and direction that will help you perform at your best. Thoughts and images are energy. You have a personal connection to an unlimited source of energy in the form of power words and high-performance images that you can use to enhance your game. Remember, attitude is a matter of choice, and you're the boss.

**A good hockey player needs the head, needs the legs, needs the hands, and needs the heart.**
*Peter Stastny, former NHL and Slovak all-star (Legends 2000)*

I want to add a power word to the list of suggestions that you received earlier. I encourage you to use the word and see if, and how, it can be useful for you. The power word I want you to add is *love.*

Love is an antidote to fear. Fear is the most limiting program that people run on their mental TVs. Fear has many faces—fear of failure, fear of embarrassment, fear of not meeting expectations, fear of letting the team down, fear of getting hurt, fear of losing control, fear of the unknown, and even fear of success. Fear causes tension, cuts down breathing, reduces energy flow, and ultimately limits performance.

Love is more powerful than fear. Love is expansive. It opens us to new possibilities. Although fear can motivate a good performance, love can inspire great performances. Love is one of the most powerful forces available to us as human beings. When we combine love with talent and training, remarkable things are possible.

Interesting? Perhaps. But does it relate to hockey? Absolutely. Love is at the core of winning hockey. It's a hockey tough concept. When Wayne Gretzky announced his retirement, he was asked what advice he had for young players starting off in the game today. Gretzky's advice was not to play hockey for whatever you might get out of it in the end, such as money or fame, but to play hockey because you love it. And to play like you love it. Good things may flow from that. That sentiment is echoed by many of the players I have worked with. Over and over they tell me that when they play with passion, they feel like a kid enjoying the game and they play their best.

Grow your passion for the game. Choose something to love in every hockey situation. Use the pressures and the challenges. Before a big game against an intimidating opponent, think: "I love the game. I love to compete. I love the challenge. I love to be pushed to be my best." Love produces energy. Fear produces *dis-ease.* To make the most of any situation you're facing, even a challenging one, choose it, use it, love it, and transform it.

Harry Neale, a former NHL head coach and GM and for many years an analyst on "Hockey Night in Canada," believes passion for the game is a quality shared by many of the game's most successful players. "The degree to which a player loves the game determines whether or not he'll be a great player," Harry told me. "A big part of Gordie Howe's greatness was his love of the game and his dedication to it. It was a passion that Howe kept alive throughout his career." Harry added, "When a player starts to think 'What am I going to do when I stop playing hockey?' there's shift in mind-set and a decrease in passion that does more to end his career than old and tired legs."

**To me, hockey always was tremendous fun. That's what kept me going. I simply love to play hockey.**

*Gordie Howe, NHL all-star and Hall of Famer*

## Feel the Love

Recall some of the hockey imagery we discussed earlier. Imagine feeling strong on your skates, moving well, making good reads, being aggressive and smooth with the puck. Imagine going into the corner against a bigger, stronger player. Imagine getting good position, being low and balanced. Imagine winning the puck. Again, love the challenge. Love beating the big men. Love dominating the smaller guys. Love being out there on the edge. Love pushing the envelope. Love making a good pass. Love to score.

Thinking love thoughts can change your feelings and make it easier to handle any challenging situation. Your passion for the game can help you tap a limitless power source. Fear stimulates action; it can kick start you to get going. Imagine a bear chasing you through the woods. You are racing ahead of it. You're frightened. You're tense. You would probably move very quickly. But the greatest performances come when people go beyond fear and move into the love zone. Again, love to skate, love to check, love to hit, love to score, love to dominate, love the challenge, love being there, love to compete, love quality competition, love pushing yourself into the unknown. Love the game.

---

The game of hockey is like a mirror. It's an opportunity to learn and to grow, to discover what you have to work on to become a more complete athlete. Many players push themselves to succeed because of their fear of failure, and they run themselves down when they don't perform well. Go beyond making failure a negative driver. It's stressful and difficult to live like that. Instead, think: "I love the challenge. I don't need to achieve something to be someone." Think "I'm OK and I'm getting better." Start by being positive about yourself and finding something to love in every hockey situation.

Hockey is a game of passion. Find things to love about the challenge you're facing and how you play the game.

# HOMEWORK

## Assignment 1: Explore Commitment

Set some goals. Set goals for the month, the week, the next game, and the next practice. See yourself working toward your goals and around any possible obstacles. One of the keys to commitment is learning how to use adversity to make you stronger.

## Assignment 2: Identity and Confidence

Take a look at your identity and confidence. Think of your strengths as a player and write them down. Consider the elements that make you effective. Note what you have to do to maintain these strengths. Develop a training program with steps and stages that will maintain your competence at the things you are good at. As you work on your program, use positive self-talk, power words, and imagery. Strengthen your identity as someone who is good.

Think of an area that you must improve as a player and write it down. Consider the elements necessary for you to be competent in this area. List the things you would have to do to improve. Develop a training schedule with steps and stages to improve in this area. As you work on your program, use positive self-talk, power words, and imagery. Bolster your identity as someone who is good.

## Assignment 3: Identity Statement

Review and edit your identity statement. Repeat it to yourself at least once a day and twice on game days. Make it a regular part of your training program and preparation.

## Assignment 4: Love of the Game

Grow your passion for the game. Choose things to love about hockey and your situation. Start to use *love* as a power word in your training. Love is one of the most powerful forces you can have working for you. Love to play. Love to train. Love to compete. Love a challenge. Love to check. Love to score. Love to compete with the big guys. Love to dominate the small guys. Love yourself. Love the situation you're in.

Continue working with all your power words and affirmations. Keep using them. Repetition builds strength. If a couple of words or statements don't feel right to you, let them go. Always be looking for new words. Add a new word or drop a word that you're not using or that doesn't seem to have power for you.

# CHAPTER
# 6

# ═══Making It═══

Almost every player I've worked with has a dream or a goal. Most want to be the best they can be and play and excel at the highest level possible.

## THE SCOUT'S POINT OF VIEW

I asked several NHL scouts and coaches what it takes to make it in the NHL, specifically, what are the psychological qualities they look for in young talent. Here's what they had to say.

Jim Nill was a tough-checking winger for several teams, including the Vancouver Canucks and Detroit Red Wings. Now an assistant general manager of the Wings, Jim has been scouting young talent for many years. He said teams look for character. They look for young players with a passion for the game, players who won't give up, no matter what obstacles get in their way. Chris Chelios, Tiger Williams, and Dave Taylor were all young players of questionable talent who went on to become NHL stars because of their determination, work ethic, and passion to compete.

Ron Delorme, another former NHL checker and now a senior scout for the Vancouver Canucks, says, "Of course we look for skating ability and size. But I also look at a player's character and his willingness to compete." When I asked Ron what he meant by character, he said, "Grit, determination, and mental toughness. It's not just about being the biggest and strongest. It's the desire to get in there and give it what you've got. That's what I look for."

Bart Bradley, a senior scout with the Boston Bruins, introduced me to the five S's that he said some scouts use to evaluate young players: skating, size, skill, sense, and spirit. He said spirit is as important as any of the others. When I asked him what he meant by spirit, he said, "Plain and simple, it's about a player's guts, his willingness to go into the corners and fight for the puck."

Mike Penny, director of player personnel for the Toronto Maple Leafs, has been evaluating young hockey talent for 30 years. Mike says what he looks for is quite simple. "Can he play or can't he play? His ability to play at an NHL level comes down to three things: his skating ability, having a good feel for the game, and not being afraid." If a player has all three of these tools, Mike says, it's a pretty sure bet he can play in the NHL. He might even make it with two of the three.

As we spoke about different players, some who had been successful and some who failed to make it, Mike added two other factors to the definition of character: work ethic and passion for the game. "Skills can be developed," Mike says, "but if a player is afraid, that doesn't change. Work ethic is something that a person grows up with, and it's also difficult to change. The young men who make it in this league are tough, reliable players who have a good work ethic and love to play. The players who won't make it in the game are the lazy guys. Few of them ever change, and they are a constant struggle for their coaches."

Frank Jay, a senior scout for the Ottawa Senators, also has been prospecting talent for decades. Frank says he looks for skating, speed, size, instincts, and toughness. Beyond those qualities, he looks for character. When I asked him what character meant to him, Frank replied, "We want to know if the kid is sincere, and if he's a good person. It's not always easy to tell, but it's very important." I asked if he meant that if he saw a player with good physical attributes, someone who was a good, tough player but wasn't a good person, he wouldn't be interested in him. "Yes," Frank said, "that's what I'm saying. I think it's important for us to select good people."

Craig Channell, a veteran scout with the Nashville Predators, described several mental strengths he looks for in assessing young prospects. "What's especially valuable is a player's ability to battle through all kinds of adversity and not let things affect him and take him off his game. It's a kind of toughness. Whether he's taking a pounding, whether the referee makes a bad call, whether it's his third travel game in three nights, or whether he has been experiencing family problems off the ice, nothing affects the player's play. He just keeps coming."

Craig also explores how a player accepts direction and criticism from the coach and uses it to become better. He's looking for someone who is determined and can adjust. He says that for many young players with ability, a determinant of their success is their willingness or drive to "push hard enough and do what they have to do to get to the next level."

Bob Berry, a pro scout and former NHL coach, echoed what all the scouts have said. "There's more to this game than skill and speed," Bob says. "I look for intensity, determination, and passion." Addressing the mental toughness the game demands, Bob quoted an old standby question that separates the men from the boys: "Do you want to play hockey or do you want to be a hockey player?"

**You can have all the talent in the world, but if the pumper's not there it doesn't matter.**

*Glen Sather, NHL General Manager,*
*Edmonton Oilers and New York Rangers (Sather 1996)*

I watched a junior game with John Chapman, the Philadelphia Flyers head scout. He was looking at a talented young winger with good skill and obvious scoring ability. "These things are important qualities," he said. "So are size and skating ability. But we also look at a player's make-up. Specifically, we want to know how he deals with pressure situations. We also try to assess a player's determination, his work ethic, and his passion for the game." A term John used to describe a player's toughness and willingness to go into the corners was *battle level*. That night the young winger's battle level could have been more impressive.

To sum up, whether it's called character, make-up, or simply attitude, the experts clearly believe there is a psychological constellation of behaviors that is vital for a player to have if he or she wants to make it to the next level. These behaviors have been described by terms such as determination, grit, guts, battle level, competitiveness, courage, drive, fight, a passion for the game, a passion to compete, a willingness to pay the price, perseverance, the ability to stay on track, coachability, and a willingness to take direction and follow instructions. These are all core qualities of success, and part of being hockey tough.

# TESTING

One thing that makes a scout's job challenging is reading a young player's potential and predicting who will mature into an NHL player. Character is a significant factor in making that determination and is not something that can be measured easily. Several NHL teams use psychological testing in an attempt to improve their selection of prospective NHL players. A test is nothing more than a standardized interview in which the responses of the player are compared with the response patterns of other athletes who have been successful or who have failed in the past.

One psychological test I have used with athletes in a variety of sports is the Athletic Success Profile (ASP).* The ASP is used by several NHL teams. It looks at 11 different factors: drive, determination, leadership, emotional control, coachability, trust, aggressiveness, responsibility, self-confidence, mental toughness, and conscientiousness. Here are the ASP's definitions of each of the 11 traits.

1. **Drive** is the desire or need to win, to achieve, and to be successful in athletics. An athlete with drive desires to attain athletic excellence and responds positively to competitive situations. He or she aspires to accomplish difficult tasks, and sets and maintains high goals in athletics.

2. **Determination** is the willingness to put forth the physical effort necessary to be successful. A determined athlete is persistent and unrelenting in work habits, practices long and hard, works on skills until exhausted, works independently, and does not give up easily on a problem.

3. **Leadership** is the desire to influence or direct others in athletics. A leader assumes the role of leader naturally and spontaneously. He or she enjoys the responsibility and challenge of being a leader and attempts to control the environment and to influence or direct others. A leader makes decisions and expresses opinions in a forceful manner.

4. **Emotional control** is the capability to maintain composure during the stress of athletic competition. An athlete with strong emotional control can face stress in a calm, objective manner. He or she rarely allows feelings to affect performance and is not easily discouraged, depressed, or frustrated by bad breaks, calls, or mistakes.

5. **Coachability** means respect for coaches and the coaching process. A coachable athlete considers coaching essential to

---

*The ASP, formerly the AMI, is currently distributed by AthleticSuccess.com.

becoming a good athlete and is receptive to coaches' advice. He or she cooperates with athletic authorities and accepts the leadership of the team captain.

6. **Trust** is the acceptance of, and belief in, people. A trusting athlete believes what coaches and fellow athletes say, is free of jealous tendencies, and tends to get along well with fellow athletes.

7. **Aggressiveness** is the belief that taking the offensive is crucial to winning. An aggressive athlete has the tendency to initiate action and to take the offensive. He or she releases aggression readily, is ready and willing to use force to get the job done, will not allow others to be pushy, and may try to get even with people.

8. **Responsibility** is the acceptance of responsibility for the consequences of one's actions, including mistakes. A responsible athlete accepts blame and criticism, even when not deserved, can endure physical and mental pain, and may dwell on mistakes and impose self-punishment.

9. **Self-confidence** is the belief that one has the ability needed to be successful in sports. A self-confident athlete has an unfaltering trust in self and feels sure of personal powers, abilities, and skills. He or she handles unexpected situations well, makes decisions with assurance, and may be quick to express beliefs, ideas, and opinions to coaches and other athletes.

10. **Mental toughness** is the ability to accept strong criticism and setbacks without competing less effectively. A mentally tough athlete does not become easily upset when losing or competing poorly, does not need excessive praise or encouragement from coaches, and recovers quickly when things go wrong.

11. **Conscientiousness** is the willingness to do things according to the rules. A conscientious athlete will not attempt to bend the rules to suit personal needs. He or she will display the tendency to be exacting in character and dominated by a sense of duty, places the good of the group ahead of personal well-being, and does not try to con the coach or other players.

Add all these factors together, put them on the ice in a high-speed contact game like hockey, and you have hockey toughness.

Players might find it useful to assess themselves with regard to each of these traits and adjust accordingly (table 6.1). If you would like more input, ask your coach or a teammate to meet with you and discuss their perception of you with regard to these qualities.

Awareness put to use is power. Become more aware of your strengths and also those character areas that you could improve to be more effective.*

---

*A player who wants a professional personal evaluation or a coach who wants a team evaluation using these traits can contact Athletic Success.com.

## Assessment

Assess yourself on each of the 11 attributes of the ASP. Estimate your hockey behavior relative to each attribute on a scale of 1 to 5, with 1 being extremely low and 5 being extremely high. If you want additional input, ask your coach to do the same and compare and discuss your findings.

After defining one or two areas in which you could improve, create a training plan to develop your strengths in these areas. For example, if you scored low on emotional control, try some of the exercises in

## Personal Assessment

| Attribute | 1 (low) | 2 | 3 (average) | 4 | 5 (high) |
|---|---|---|---|---|---|
| Drive | | | | | |
| Determination | | | | | |
| Leadership | | | | | |
| Emotional control | | | | | |
| Coachability | | | | | |
| Trust | | | | | |
| Aggressiveness | | | | | |
| Responsibility | | | | | |
| Self-confidence | | | | | |
| Mental toughness | | | | | |
| Conscientiousness | | | | | |

chapter 2. If determination is an area you want to improve, work on goal setting. Set a goal for the season, for each month and week, and for each practice. Write down your goals and repeat them to yourself often. Then see that you do the work necessary to achieve the goals you've set.

---

The qualities of character that professional scouts refer to most frequently are commitment, determination, passion for the game, and mental toughness. These are the mental software programs they are searching for in future NHL stars. We discussed commitment and passion in chapter 5. In the next part of this chapter, I will talk about mental toughness.

# HOCKEY TOUGHNESS
# IS MENTAL TOUGHNESS

In an aggressive, physical, high-speed, collision sport like hockey, with many games and much travel, a special kind of mental toughness is demanded—what I call hockey toughness.

Hockey toughness means many things.

It's knowing what to do and working hard to make it happen.

It's the ability to deal with pressure and mistakes and not lose confidence or heart.

It's being prepared.

It's playing hard and putting the team first.

It's respecting your teammates.

It's having discipline and control.

It's skating away from an enticement to retaliate.

It's blocking shots.

It's winning the puck on the boards with a bigger player bearing down on you.

It's going for the pass in front of the net knowing a defenseman is about to cross-check you.

It's being relentless.

It's pushing yourself to be the best you can be.

It's using it.

It's going the extra mile, even when you are tired.

It's battling back from injury.

It's focusing on solutions and not complaining.

It's an unwillingness to ease up when down by two goals or up by two goals.

It's tuning out or parking what's negative.

It's playing like every shift will decide the outcome of the game.

It's staying focused on the goal—winning the game.

In a close game, down by a goal with the man advantage, when someone cheap shots you, instead of retaliating (and possibly losing a power-play opportunity), it's staying focused on working to generate a scoring opportunity for your team.

Billy Smith, the former New York Islanders' goalie who is now an NHL coach, was a mentally tough competitor. When I asked him about staying focused and playing tough, he told me that if you're going to play tough, you have to keep control. He said, "I never retaliated. I always initiated. There's a big difference." Reminiscing about the 1981-82 Stanley Cup finals, Billy said, "We [the Islanders] had an understanding not to retaliate and not to fight. And we didn't. Even when Tiger Williams ripped the chain right off my neck, I wouldn't fight. The Canucks did. They took the penalties and we scored the goals."

Duane Sutter, another NHL veteran player and coach, agrees with Smith's dictum about initiating and not retaliating. "Al Arbour [a former all-star NHL defenseman and successful NHL coach] used to say, 'If you're ready to play, you initiate. If you're not ready, you end up playing from behind all night long.'"

Hockey toughness is expressed in your consistent determination to do what's necessary and your focus to get it done, no matter what the situation: if you're a scorer and haven't scored in several games, if you're a checker or a defenseman and your check gets open in front of the net and scores, or if you've been benched or are getting little ice time. In each situation, hockey toughness is that quality that won't let you get down on yourself, your teammates, or the coach, but instead encourages you to stay positive and work hard to exhibit your ability and reach your goal.

I asked Jack McIlhargey, a veteran NHL defenseman and a coach with the Vancouver Canucks, about hockey toughness. Jack said,

"It's not letting things get to you. If you make a mistake on the ice, don't dwell on it. Mental toughness is that ability to stay focused on the positive."

In practice, mental toughness might manifest itself as follows. Imagine you're tired. You've had a number of games recently, and you feel it. Practice is over, but ice time is available, and you are determined to improve your skating. So instead of hanging with the guys, you stay on the ice and do extra work with power skating exercises to improve your conditioning or to develop into the player you want to become.

Hockey toughness is mind over matter. Chris Pronger described it as "having that feeling that your legs are just too tired and still working hard and toughing it out." He added, "You won't believe how mental it is."

Hockey toughness in practice is regularly taking an extra half hour to work on improving the accuracy of your shot. Hockey toughness is working on the things you aren't good at and don't particularly enjoy. Hockey toughness is expressed in discipline and hard work over the summer months and doing more than just the required training so that you come into camp in excellent shape.

Following injury, hockey toughness is the ability to focus on climbing back up the mountain and not surrendering to the frustration and disappointment that follows lost opportunity, lost conditioning, and the pain and sweat necessary to get you back where you want to be. It's following your rehabilitation program and moving forward one step at a time (see chapter 12).

Mattias Ohlund came into training camp for his third year in the NHL in exceptional shape. He had worked very hard all summer on his conditioning and had an exceptional camp. Then, in the team's fifth preseason exhibition game, he was struck directly in the eye by a puck from a slapshot traveling 90-plus miles an hour. It was a serious injury. There was considerable internal bleeding in the eye and concern that Mattias might lose his sight in that eye. He was ordered to rest completely for a month to minimize the possibility of further hemorrhaging. It was difficult for this motivated player, who had just spent 12 weeks training intensively to get into the best shape in his life, to simply do nothing. But it had to be done. And it was done without complaint.

Then the slow road back began, including rest, surgery on the eye, more rest, medication, then after two months, small steps such as going for a walk, monitored light training in the gym, more intensive training, then on-ice training—light at first, still no contact—and finally some contact drills, then full contact. Four months after the injury, Mattias was back in the lineup, not in the ideal shape he had been in at the start of the season, but still expected to handle the speed and pressure of playing defense in the NHL and to play great hockey. In his first game back, he played more than 20 minutes. His ice time jumped to 30 minutes two games after that. He struggled with conditioning at first and was criticized in the press, but not once throughout that entire process did I ever hear Mattias complain or offer an excuse. By the end of the year, he was playing excellent hockey. That's mental toughness.

One characteristic that underlies hockey toughness is a commitment to excellence. After Mattias returned to form, I spoke with him about his mental toughness. Not surprisingly, he played it down. Mattias said, "One thing that helped me was a conversation we had when I was first coming back after my injury. I wasn't playing as well as I knew I was capable of, and it bothered me. You gave me some perspective when you said, 'You may not be at your best, but you are still playing well. You can't expect to be outstanding if you are not in excellent shape and your vision is less than perfect. Just do what you can for now.' I knew I was doing the best I could. You helped me to reduce my expectations and take some pressure off myself."

Mario Lemieux, one of the greatest players of all time, is the embodiment of hockey toughness. His brilliance, determination, skill, and passion to play have led his teams to Stanley Cup victories and Olympic gold. In the process, Mario has been challenged by some of the most extreme forms of adversity. At the height of his career, Mario battled back from cancer to win the scoring title and the NHL's most valuable player award. Then he experienced years of intense, debilitating back pain that caused him to miss an entire season. Again, without complaint, he battled back to star.

Of the latter period, Mario said, "Well, the back pain was pretty intense for a couple of years, to the point where I couldn't tie my shoes and I couldn't tie my skates. We had one of our trainers come in before every game and tie my skates. That's how I got on the ice." He added, "I remember for a couple of years I very seldom practiced. I just played games" (*Legends* 2000). And he starred.

Being sent to the minors can challenge one's mental toughness. Trent Klatt was an NHL veteran who scored more than 20 goals in a season playing with the Philadelphia Flyers' top line. Then, after a disappointing season and a half with the Vancouver Canucks, he was sent down to the AHL. The move down was difficult for someone who had been a respected NHLer. What made it even more difficult was that Trent's family had to be uprooted and relocated. Many pros would have become negative. Trent didn't. He viewed the assignment as an opportunity and used it.

Trent worked very hard in the AHL. He regained his scoring touch, overcame a painful foot injury, and because of his excellent play, earned himself another opportunity with the Canucks. When he returned to the Canucks' lineup, he played extremely well. For the rest of the season and into the next, he was one of the team's hardest-working players in every game and on every shift. Nothing seemed to distract him.

I saw Trent's ability to use the situation rather then letting it use him as an example of hockey toughness and of a player using his mind to turn things around. When I asked him about it, he said, "I love to play hockey, both offense and defense. But when I was here, I began worrying about defense, just defense. I let things distract me, and the game stopped being fun. When I was sent down, I was determined to use the opportunity to refocus and play like I knew I could play. That meant becoming more aggressive on offense, making things happen, staying positive, and having fun. So I did."

Hockey toughness is being ready and able to play your best hockey whether you make the A team or are sent to the B team. After a good training camp, Vic was sent to the NHL team's AHL affiliate. He played well, and when a few NHL players were injured, he was called up to the NHL team. Again Vic played well, scored a few goals, and impressed the NHL coaches. When he was sent back down to the AHL, he continued to play well. Not surprisingly, Vic was called back up the next time the injury bug hit the NHL team. Again he played well. Eventually, he was sent back down and played well. When I asked Vic about the experience of going up and down so many times and living out of a suitcase, he said, "It wasn't easy. Sometimes I woke up and I wasn't sure where I was. But I can't control the moves. I want to play. And my only focus is preparing myself to play well." That's hockey toughness.

In contrast, Paul, a talented young player, was assigned to an AHL team after a good NHL training camp. He was disappointed with the assignment, and his play suffered. He took a while to adjust and pick up his game. Finally, his game improved and he was called up to the NHL team. He played a few games and was sent down. Again he was upset and disappointed. Again his play suffered.

Hockey toughness is expressed in getting up to compete hard every day throughout the long hockey season. When I asked Scott Gomez how he was adjusting to his rookie year in the NHL, he said, "One of the things that's important is to stay focused. There's so much happening, so much positive and negative energy. You have to know how to handle it. Whether you've had a good game or a bad game, you have to be able to psyche yourself, especially at this top level. I try not to get too high or too low. Sure, I celebrate a little when I score, but then it's back to focusing on what you've got to do on your next shift or in your next game. What's helped me so far is going back to my breathing and thinking positively and thinking about my ABCs."

Hockey toughness is about all of the above. Mental toughness is disciplined, focused, positive, goal-directed behavior. Some say it's a quality that can't be taught—either you are born mentally tough or you are not. I don't agree. Early experience and upbringing are undoubtedly big factors in developing mental toughness; however, mental toughness is about focus, and focus is something you can control. You can make yourself mentally tougher by working on the following six skill areas:

1. **Set goals.** To be mentally tough, recognize that you are *response-able* and know what you want. Have a clear sense of direction and purpose. Define your goal(s). It's much easier to stay focused and on course if you have a course to stay on. Know where you are going. Know your purpose and goal.

2. **Become an expert at mastering your emotions.** Learn how to change channels and stay centered. That means release, breathe, and refocus on what you want to make happen in any situation.

3. **Use positive imagery.** Create positive pictures of where you are going and what you want to do on the ice. Create success images that support your motivation and drive. Use mental rehearsal to increase your focus and competence. Be a tiger, panther, or bear. Build a powerful, positive self-image that will help you play winning hockey and realize your goal.

4. **Use positive self-talk.** Say positive things to yourself. Acknowledge your effort and your successes. Use your challenges and difficulties. Positive self-talk will help you to succeed and stay on track.

5. **Be willing to work hard and be in great shape.** Fatigue makes us vulnerable to doubt. Being in great shape builds confidence and supports the positive focus and determination that are the building blocks of mental toughness. Dave "Tiger" Williams, one of the NHL's toughest guys, attests to the importance of preparation and superconditioning to sustain confidence and stay on task. Dave told me, "When you get fitness tested, work to be in the top percentile of your team. It will help you to keep going and give you a greater chance to succeed." Dave, who played for Toronto, Vancouver, Detroit, Los Angeles, and Hartford, added, "If you are traded from a good team to a bad team, it can be very difficult to get up and stay positive when your chances of winning each night seem remote. But mental toughness is about playing hard every night, on every shift, on every team. And conditioning and commitment make that more possible."

6. **Grow a winning attitude.** Be a pro. Be committed to using everything. Whatever comes up, use it, learn from it, dominate it. Grow your confidence with preparation. Grow your identity as someone who is determined. And grow your passion for the game.

## CHANGE THE CHANNEL

Some sport psychologists have used the concept of *parking* to describe the experience of tuning out irrelevant thoughts and staying tuned into what's appropriate. If a thought comes to mind that's not going to help you perform or can interfere with your on-ice performance, change the channel and park it.

For example, if an opposition player taunts you, slashes you, or attempts to provoke or distract you in a close game, instead of retaliating and hurting your team, park that thought and possibly file it for later. If it's something that can't be forgotten, then at another time, when it won't hurt your team, even the score. If you are having distracting or disturbing thoughts relating to off-ice issues and it's time to prepare for the game, park those thoughts for the time being and deal with them later.

Parking requires both perspective and emotional control, qualities of mental toughness. Your ability to tune out a thought, change channels, and park it is a combination of your motivation and your ability to release, breathe, and refocus.

Paul Kariya is an intensely focused, hockey tough competitor who knows his role and what it takes to be successful. When I asked Paul how he dealt with the high sticks, late hits, clutch and grabs, and other frustrations in the game today, he replied, "Getting angry doesn't accomplish anything. It doesn't help me score." Paul explained, "When I was in the Canadian national junior program, a sport psychologist introduced the idea of parking it, and it's something I still use today. I'm an offensive player. My job is to play offense. It's not to retaliate. If someone chops or slashes me, I park it and refocus. The ultimate get-even is to put the puck in their net."

One of my favorite examples of mental discipline, and something I'm fond of telling young hockey players, is: "When I walk through my neighborhood and my neighbor's dog barks, I don't bark back." I have said this dozens of times. Usually, most players smile and nod. They can appreciate that it's ridiculous to bark back at a dog.

On the ice, however, when someone on the other team barks at them, many players lose perspective and focus and bark back. My advice is, don't go there. Ignore it. If you do notice the provocation, use it or it'll use you. How can you use it? As always, take

Paul Kariya doesn't let the frustrations of the competitive game pull him away from his focus on being an offensive player. After a devestating hit in game 6 of the 2003 Stanley Cup finals, Kariya bounced back to lead the Anaheim Mighty Ducks, forcing a decisive game 7 against the New Jersey Devils.

© SportsChrome

a breath, release (anger, tension, frustration, fear, or whatever), and focus instead on the positive—what you want to do on the ice (your ABCs). Mental toughness is about maintaining that positive focus, no matter what.

Mike Johnson, an NHL coach, said, "People who are mentally tough are resilient. They always believe they are going to find a way to do it, and they keep working to make it happen." These people draw heavily on positive past experiences. They've done it before, and they know they can and will do it again. Explained this way, you can see that mental toughness is closely related to confidence and, like confidence, flows from success. Mike went on to say, "That's why teams like to have successful veterans, winners, on the team. Their confidence and mental toughness have a positive impact on others."

## HOCKEY TOUGH IS HOCKEY SMART

Hockey tough is hockey smart. I have seen players do things thinking they were being hockey tough and making a statement for the team or for pride when in reality what they were doing was neither hockey tough nor hockey smart.

Mark was a hard-working junior defenseman. Although he wasn't big, he was a fearless, physical player who would stand up to anyone to protect his teammates. The problem was that Mark didn't control his temper. On the ASP, he was strong on drive and aggressiveness but low on emotional control. In the second period of a close game, with his team leading 1-0, Mark was speared. He retaliated and was given a two-minute penalty. Not surprisingly, he was upset. Thirty seconds after Mark went to the penalty box, the other team scored a power-play goal. As Mark left the penalty box (still steaming), one of the opposing players skated by and said something to the effect that Mark was a dummy who'd just cost his team a goal. Mark snapped. He jumped the opponent and started throwing punches. When the smoke cleared, Mark was back in the penalty box all by himself with a two-minute penalty for instigating the fight and a five-minute penalty for fighting. The complexion of the game shifted.

Clearly, it's counterproductive to work hard and stand up for your teammates and out of control. Hockey tough means playing smart hockey with discipline and not allowing your emotions (right brain) to override your focus (left brain).

Mick was a feisty 17-year-old winger on a junior team who thought he was a tough guy. A couple of days before a four-games-in-four-nights road trip, Mick went to a local cinema with several of his teammates. At the theater, he started chatting with a young woman he met in the lobby. After a few minutes, he noticed two young men glaring at him. "Do you have a problem?" he asked them. They said they did. Apparently, the young woman was the girlfriend of one of their friends. "Well, then, let's go outside," snapped Mick. Mick led the two young men outside into the theater parking lot, where they soundly beat him up, knocking out a couple of his teeth and cutting his face, requiring several stitches. Although Mick tried to play, the injury prevented him from participating in any of his team's four games.

As we sat in the stands, I explained to Mick that he had let his teammates down. "How's that?" he asked. "Well," I replied, "you're a good two-way player. You check and you can score. And here you are sitting in the stands with me while your teammates are out there battling on the ice. That's not being a good team player." He understood and said he hadn't thought of it like that. Then he added, "But these guys challenged me. I had to fight them. It was a matter of pride." I explained to Mick that being hockey tough means maintaining a team focus and discipline and doing what serves the team on and off the ice. "Real toughness is not responding to every barking dog. It's having a clear focus and acting with purpose, intelligence, and control in the face of challenge and adversity."

# CHAPTER 7

# Playing a Winning Team Game

Hockey is the ultimate team game. I have worked with teams in the NHL, NFL, NBA, and major-league baseball. In my opinion, players on a good hockey team are closer and more interdependent during the game than players in any of the other major sports. Part of the reason is the nature of the game. Hockey is an intense contact sport that bonds players together. Hockey is also a high-speed, lateral-flow game. Hockey success comes from everyone working together and moving the puck from player to player. Puck movement generates scoring opportunities.

One of my favorite stories is about Roger Neilson lining players up on the blue line at practice and telling each line to skate as fast as they could to the far end of the rink. When he said "Go," the first line sprinted down the ice as fast as they could. When they reached the far blue line, Roger fired a puck at the end boards. The puck beat the players to the end boards. Then he said "Go" again and the second line took off at full speed. Once more, he waited until they hit the far blue line and fired the puck, which beat the players to the end boards. He repeated the same thing with the third and fourth lines. Always the puck got there first. The players asked, "Rog, what's the point, the puck's always going to get there first?" "Exactly," replied Neilson. "The puck travels faster than you can skate. If you want to make something happen, pass the puck."

Hockey is a game of flow. It is also a very physical game. Another expression of the team closeness the game generates is the way teammates stand up for each other.

What is a team? The definition I like best is a team is a group of animals hitched together pulling in a common direction toward a common goal, like a dog team or a team of horses. Seen in this manner, it's dramatically clear that if one of the dogs or horses stops pulling or pulls in another direction, the rest of the team must pull harder.

Success in hockey comes from everyone pulling together. It's about players understanding their roles, working together, executing the game plan, and respecting and supporting each other.

In hockey, the "we" must be greater than the "me." It's a significant challenge for a coach to energize, enroll, direct, and mold a diverse and talented collection of individuals with different wants, goals, and personality styles into a working team. It's also a challenge for players to surrender their egos and individuality for the team's good. But that's what it takes to win.

## GREAT COACHES ON WINNING TEAMS

When I asked Scotty Bowman, the winningest coach in NHL history, what makes a winning team, he replied, "One of the greatest challenges for a coach is molding a group of players to play together and to depend on each other. No player can stand alone. It's hard for one guy, even a great player, to do it by himself. It's even hard for two good players. It's hard to have all the pressure on a couple of guys."

Hockey is a team game. Six players are on the ice at a time, and they have to work together. It's the team working together that wins. Scotty went on to say, "The team concept is very important. A team has to have some kind of identity." Two key ingredients he described as being critical to team success are players knowing their jobs and having a collective willingness to work hard. Scotty added that it is important that the better players on the team perceive themselves as stronger when they play together and model an excellent work ethic.

Phil Jackson, the repeat NBA championship coach of the Chicago Bulls and Los Angeles Lakers, wrote something similar about winning in his book *Sacred Hoops* (Jackson and Delehanty 1995).

Jackson mused that the Bulls became a championship team when Michael Jordan (with Coach Jackson's help) realized that the great player is the one who makes the players around him better. A team can only succeed when everyone is committed to playing the team game.

Vince Lombardi, the legendary and often-quoted NFL football coach, was asked by Lee Iacocca, a great corporate coach, what he thought were the keys to a winning team (Iacocca 1984). Lombardi's answer is true for hockey as well as football. He said three things make a winning team:

1. Players have to know their jobs. In hockey, that means the players know what to do on the ice. They know the system, the game plan, their role, and their ABCs.

2. The "we" is bigger than the "me." Hockey is the ultimate team game. To win, players have to be willing to commit to serving the team and executing the team's game plan as opposed to their own agenda.

3. Players must love one another.

Lombardi mused that the reason the Green Bay Packers were NFL champions was because the players loved one another. When I relate that to players, I sometimes get a strange response. Lombardi didn't mean that the players had to like one another. He meant that the players had to respect each other, stand up for each other, and maintain a standard of play that reflected that respect.

Respect is the winger going hard into the corner and winning the puck to feed the center, who is fighting for position in front of the net. It's the defenseman blocking shots or fighting to clear the front of the net to give the goalie a better chance to see and stop the puck. When the shared vision of the team is that everyone works the plan and gives 100 percent each and every shift, the team becomes successful.

I asked Scott Mellanby, NHL veteran, all-star, team captain, and team player, what constituted a winning team. Scott reiterated what Jackson and Lombardi said and related it to hockey. "Hockey is a team game, and you simply can't win with one or two players. I've been to the Stanley Cup finals with two different teams. In both cases, we had a strong leadership group of five or six guys who could have been captains. You must have a core of character guys."

When we discussed Phil Jackson's notion that the great player is the one who makes the players around him better, Scott agreed. "Respect is vital. I've been an all-star and a fourth-liner. I think it's really important, and I know how it feels when your stars and first-line players show respect for your third- and fourth-line guys and make them feel an important part of the team. If your top guys believe in those players, it will be easier for them to believe in themselves. And it's those third- and fourth-line guys that have to score for you in the playoffs for you to win."

Scott mentioned that sometimes in practice, a star and a fourth-liner are paired in doing two-on-one drills. He said it's important for the star to make the fourth-liner feel that he believes in his ability and to be positive and work hard with him. "I have seen first-liners who do just that, and then there are those head hangers who send the message 'You are not good enough to drill with me.' And that kind of thing has a real negative impact on a team." Scott added, "A team needs character guys, and a player's true character emerges in the hard times. It's easy to be a good guy when things are going your way."

I recall Mike Keenan reminiscing about the successful Canada Cup team he coached. Part of the team's success was that the players (NHL all-stars) had an incredibly supportive feeling for each other. They respected each other and were willing to do what it took to support their teammates. Mike said, "It was something you could feel when you walked into the room."

Of course, that feeling of oneness and support is not always there on talent-loaded teams, and sometimes it manifests itself with teams that are down but not quite out. I've observed teams in the NHL and WHL that were down in the standings, missing five of their top players due to injury, and scheduled to play the league's top team come together, step up their game, play for each other, and successfully overachieve.

Another thing Lombardi said that applies to hockey as well as football is about effort. Lombardi said that a football game may have 50 to 60 plays but only three or four are game-breakers that determine the outcome of the game. *You have to play every play as if it's the one that is going to make the difference.* It's the same in hockey. A player may have 20 or 30 shifts in a game and only one or two shifts may be game-breakers. You have to play as if every shift is going to make the difference. There's an old saying, "On a team, everyone makes a difference." I often ask players, "What kind of a difference do you make? Will it be one that adds to the team or one that detracts from it? It's your choice." A hockey tough player is a team player.

When the Vancouver Canucks had their training camp in Kamloops, British Columbia, home of the perennial Memorial Cup champion Kamloops Blazers (WHL), I noticed some advice posted on the wall of the Blazers' dressing room. It's good team advice and, if followed, could explain part of the Blazers success. It's called the Blazers Code of Commitment:

- To prepare every day as best we can
- To play with discipline every shift
- To support each other every shift
- To never let ourselves be outworked
- To follow the game plan to the best of our ability
- To pay the price necessary to win

These team directives are designed to help individuals play as a team and win at a team game. One more Blazer tidbit: On the door of the Blazers' dressing room is a sign that reads: "The name on the front of the jersey is more important than the one on the back."

Steve Yzerman, a perennial all-star and an exemplary captain who has led the Detroit Red Wings to several Stanley Cups, offered a succinct statement of his philosophy of leadership and team play: "I always try to do what is best for the team." Any player would do well to display that phrase in his or her locker.

When I asked Steve to elaborate, he said, "You play a team sport. You didn't choose to play tennis or some other individual sport. So you have to put the best interests of the team ahead of your own. Generally, things will work out for you, individually, if you have that attitude. You may not lead the league in scoring, but that's not important. In team sports, winning is the most important thing. It's the number-one goal. Do your best in the role you're given."

Like Steve Yzerman, Joe Thornton was a young superstar when he was appointed captain of his team the Boston Bruins. Both Joe and Steve initially were challenged to lead teams that had a number of older, more experienced players. Both said they adopted a leadership style of leading by example and exhibiting good work habits on the ice rather than talking it up in the locker room. When I asked Joe what he thought of Yzerman's leadership philosophy—"I always try to do what is best for the team"—he nodded in agreement and said, "A team is like a locomotive. To get it rolling, everybody has to work together and everybody has to play his role. Then it can become a powerful force."

Pat Quinn has been an NHL coach of the year for three different teams. When I asked Pat how to build a winning team, he said, "You begin with what you've got. If possible, you set up a model with strength down the middle. It starts in goal. Good goaltending creates a confidence for the people up front. Center is the key position to the transition game. No team wins the cup without strength at center."

For over two decades, Mark Messier has been a beacon of strength at center. Mark has helped win six Stanley Cups and led two teams to the ultimate hockey championship. "You need good players to win, but winning is more than that," said Mark. "There's a certain kind of feeling, an expectation of success that's part of a winning team. It develops on different teams for different reasons. On some teams, there's so much talent and skill you just know you're good and that you can and will be successful. The Edmonton Oilers [of the 1980s] were like that. And it was fun to be a part of that."

Mark also talked about the New York Rangers team he led to the Stanley Cup in 1994. He said the experience and strong feeling of leadership on that team created a positivity and confidence that permeated the room and the team. "On teams without as much talent and experience as those teams, a certain belief in the team comes about by working hard together. You can create a winning mind-set by playing a solid team game. It's important that all the players believe that they contribute and that they make a difference. Whether a guy plays 30 minutes or 5 minutes, whether he's a scorer or a checker, when everyone believes they make a difference and play like they make a difference, remarkable things can happen. I've seen it."

I asked Marc Crawford, a Stanley Cup-winning coach, about the process of building a winning team. Essentially, what Marc said applies to developing a winning team as well as a successful player. "First, you have to assess what you've got in terms of talent and character. You have to become aware of your strengths and deficiencies and build from there. If there is a void in an area, whether it's talent, character, or leadership, the void must be filled, and the talent you have must be developed."

When I asked Marc about the process of developing talent, he said, "You have to instruct your players. We do it by talking with them and using video to increase their awareness, sense of responsibility, and confidence. Last, you have to provide some feedback to the players on how they are doing. This feedback should be more positive than negative."

To develop, a player must first assess where he is. He must become aware of his strengths and deficiencies. Then he must adjust. He does that by setting goals as to the skills and strengths he wants to develop and then working hard. A positive focus is important when developing skills. That involves using positive self-talk and positive imagery (described in chapters 2 and 3). Last, a player must reflect and critique (reassess) his on-ice performance and acknowledge his successes, as well as the things he must improve.

Hockey tough is a commitment to continuous improvement. Assessing and adjusting is an ongoing process. Do it yourself. Do it with the help of teammates or a coach.

## Team Feedback

An exercise that has been used by university and junior hockey teams is to ask each player to write a brief comment about each of his teammates with regard to both what each player positively contributes to the team on and off the ice and what each player can improve or strengthen to enhance the team's performance.

The coach facilitating the exercise must make it clear that comments should be respectful of the players, the team, and the exercise. The idea is to provide players with honest feedback from their peers that acknowledge and support a player's strengths and efforts and also direct and encourage him to work more diligently on areas where he can contribute more.

Papers are filled out anonymously, then collected, shuffled, and handed back to the players. One by one, each player listens to his teammates read the comments of their peers with regard to his performance. The exercise can also be quite effective if just done among team leaders.

In one exercise with a dozen veterans and team leaders, I heard the group tell the team's leading scorer that he had to contribute more defensively, tell a star player that he had to have more discipline and that the retaliation penalties he took were hurting the team, and also tell an underconfident grinder that his hard work was appreciated and he shouldn't be so hard on himself.

A quicker, less intense approach to the same process is to pair up teammates at a team meeting and ask one of the pair to concisely describe one thing that's been most positive about his partner's contribution to the team and one thing his partner can improve or do more of to enhance team success. Then the other player is asked to do the same. The team can go around the room in 15 minutes and generate some positive peer feedback. What's essential to making this process work is a genuine desire to improve team play and an attitude of respect for teammates and the game.

---

# IMPROVING TEAMWORK

What can a player do to improve teamwork?

First, know your job. If you are not clear, ask the coaches. Understand what your linemates or defensive partners think and expect and then do it.

Second, communicate. Have a clear, positive focus about what you want to do on the ice (clear ABCs). The players around you will respond to your focus and action. For example, if the center knows that a winger will work hard in the corner to win the puck and then pass it to the front of the net, the center will do what's necessary to get to the front of the net to make the play. Similarly, if the winger knows the center will work hard to be free in front, he will work hard to get the puck to him. Talk with your teammates. Each player being clear about what he has to do and making the effort to do it will have an impact on his teammates. Be positive. Think positive and talk positive. Encourage and acknowledge the positive effort of your teammates.

Winning teams are about a commitment to team play, to the game plan, and to each other. Model a winning attitude. Work hard in practice to improve your skills, to bring a high quality and tempo to drills, and to model a winning work ethic.

Improve your conditioning and your off-ice lifestyle (diet and rest) so you can keep executing shift after shift, game after game.

To play hockey well, surrender the "me" for the greater "we." When the game is played at its best, you will get back more than you give up, plus you will have the satisfaction of being a part of something greater than yourself. A quote from Mark Messier posted on the wall of the WHL Kelowna Rockets' dressing room reminds the players of this point: "If everybody can find a way to put their personal agendas aside for the benefit of the team, ultimately they will gain for themselves in the long run. But I think what often happens is people think they have to take care of themselves first and the team second. Then the infrastructure breaks down and nobody's accountable. You have to sacrifice yourself for the good of the team, no matter what role you play on the team, whether you're playing 30 minutes or 2 minutes a game."

# BE CONSISTENT, BE PREPARED

According to coach Roger Neilson, one of the qualities necessary to being a star player that is sometimes overlooked is consistency. Roger feels preparation is key to being consistent. He said one of the most important things to learn is how to get yourself ready to play day after day, game in and game out, throughout the long season. When I asked Roger how a player might go about doing that, he said, "If a team has a hockey system, the coach's task is to get the players to play the system. Playing the system creates order, and that provides consistency. The same is true on a personal preparation level. It's having your own system and knowing what you have to do to execute on the ice, and focusing on that. It's also knowing how to prepare for games and running your routine day after day throughout the season."

Preparation is a key to confidence and success. Throughout the book are suggestions on how to prepare. Let's review five things you can do to prepare.

## Set Goals

First, set goals for the kind of player you want to become. Then set goals for what you do on the ice and in the gym. When you step onto the ice for practice, think, "Today I'm really going to work on _____ or to make _____ happen."

Train weaknesses and play strengths. Most players like to look good. Consequently, they tend to practice what they are good at and are less inclined to work on some of their weaker qualities.

Experienced junior coaches such as Gary Davidson have observed that some of the young talents that blossomed under their coaching were the players who set goals and worked hard to make themselves better by focusing on their weaknesses as well as their strengths. Davidson, who coached the Kariya brothers in the BCHL, said that two of the things that differentiated Paul and Steve were their ability to identify the things they had to improve and their intense work ethic and willingness to work on weaknesses.

I asked Steve Kariya about Davidson's assessment, and he replied, "If you want to play in the NHL, you have to develop all your abilities, the whole package. To do that you have to practice the things you are not good at. There are guys in junior who just keep taking those big slap shots in practice that they rarely have the time and space to use in the NHL."

Davidson also noted that the Kariyas were positive and practical. They didn't dwell on things they couldn't control, such as size. Instead, they maximized their quickness and strength. Davidson recalled the first year that he coached Paul Kariya as a junior. At the end of the season, the 16-year-old asked his coach what he needed to work on to improve. Davidson advised him to focus on his shot, specifically on a quick release and accuracy. Davidson said, "I don't know how many thousand of shots he took over the summer, but when he came back in the fall, it was clear that he dedicated himself to the task because Paul's shot was quicker, more accurate, and a lot more powerful." The fact that Paul has become a prolific goal scorer and an NHL shot leader is a testament to the value of commitment, talent, and hard work.

Larry Robinson, a perennial NHL all-star and a successful NHL coach, made a similar point when I asked him how he would help a player develop. "Get him to focus on his weaknesses, not his strengths. Most athletes focus on their strengths. It's human nature to focus on what you're good at and what comes easily to you. If it's easier to turn right, then people go to the right. In terms of their development, it's important to get them to do what they have trouble doing."

Donald Brashear also has a similar perspective about what it takes to improve. "There's a part of the game that comes natural to me: being the enforcer and playing physical. I don't need to focus on that. I focus more on things that are harder for me. That way, I improve on these things. The other things I know I'll do well."

## Have a Clear Focus—Know Your Job

Another thing you can do to prepare yourself to play is to create clear focus. Understand the game plan and know what you are expected to do on the ice in a variety of game situations. Discuss any uncertainties with a coach. Go over your ABCs. Use mental rehearsal to see yourself performing well. With mental practice, your reactions become more automatic.

I spoke to Chris Pronger of the St. Louis Blues about optimal pregame preparation. His response was sensible. He spoke about doing visualization and creating a positive frame of mind. "Preparation is a personal matter. Some players start preparing the morning of the game. Others start in the afternoon, and still others don't prepare until right before the game. A player should find out what works for him, then do it before every game."

Along with imagery, be aware of your thinking. Be a positive self-talker. Remember to change the channel or park any negative thoughts. Stay on your positive power channel. Before, during, and after the game, talk positively to yourself and your teammates. Acknowledge your ability and affirm your successes and their successes.

## Power Up Your Attitude

A third thing you can do to prepare is strengthen your winning attitude. Remember your goals and personal commitment to use everything to be a better player and person. Confidence grows with preparation. Know that you are physically and mentally prepared. Know that you have the energy, the skill, and the determination to execute your ABCs. (If not, work to improve your training program.) See yourself executing well. Know that's who you are. Reinforce your identity as someone who knows his job and can be counted on to make the play. Remember, hockey is an exciting game. It's a high-speed challenge on ice. Allow yourself to enjoy it.

## Create the Right Feelings

Another thing you can do to prepare is learn how to create the right feelings. In many leagues, from bantam on up, there are simply too many games. When players are tired, they make mistakes, get frustrated, and lose confidence and heart.

One key to being consistent is learning to manage energy effectively and to make sure your body gets what it needs to perform. That means eating intelligently and getting enough quality rest. Choose foods that will energize you and help you perform well. Most experts recommend a diet loaded with complex carbohydrates but only a moderate amount of protein. Avoid a hollow junk food pregame meal. Discover if there are certain foods that help or hinder your performance. Keep a record of what you eat in a performance journal and see if there is any relationship to game performance.

Get some rest. It's been said that "Fatigue makes cowards of us all." Tiredness certainly doesn't lead to consistent high-level performance. When it comes to rest, use your common sense. If you are tired, take the time to rest and recharge. I describe techniques for recharging in chapter 12.

## Put It Together

Matt was a motivated and talented junior player. He was being recruited by several college coaches and was told that a couple of scouts would be watching his next game. He wanted to make a good impression, but, although he tried hard, Matt didn't have one of his A games. The next day we talked about his performance. He described how during the previous game he had been flying around the ice, hitting everything that moved, scoring, and setting up teammates for goals. Then he said, "Last night I just wasn't sharp." He paused, shook his head, and asked, "Why can't I play every night like I did in the game before?"

I explained to Matt what I described in chapter 1, that feelings affect thinking. One of the great limiters is fear. Pressure to perform can cause nervousness or anxiety, which is fear in Matt's case. For many athletes, fear of failure leads to trying too hard and thinking too much. Trying too hard and overthinking cause tension, and tension negatively affects coordination and timing.

I suggested to Matt that he use the experience to become a better manager of his feelings. I reminded him that consistency comes from developing a good pregame routine, including good practice, good personal habits, clear focus, and the ability to stay smooth. Since Matt was a thoughtful player, I suggested he do some imagery and self-talk and then *relax*. He was given the following routine:

First, relax. Review your game focus (ABCs).

Second, see yourself playing well, offensively and defensively.

Third, affirm that you are a good player and that you will do well in the game.

Fourth, just relax. Forget about hockey. Do some breathing, have a nap, go for a walk, listen to music. Relax.

Understand that your mental computer is loaded with positive thoughts and images. Under pressure, you'll do fine and react naturally and effectively if you relax.

I shared with Matt Steve Yzerman's comments about pregame preparation: "The best thing you can do is relax, take it easy, and you'll be more energetic, as opposed to getting yourself all fired up and coming out on the first shift at 100 miles per hour. It's all downhill from there. Being relaxed, you conserve a lot more energy and your skills take over, and you rise to the importance of the situation instead of trying to build yourself up to it."

Everyone is different. Get in touch with who you are and the emotions and arousal level that facilitate your performance. Assess and adjust. If you tend to be too nervous, tense, or intense, learn to relax and calm yourself down. If you find there are times when you are flat, learn how to energize and pump yourself up. If you have trouble controlling your temper and take costly, selfish retaliation penalties, learn to change channels and manage your emotions. Develop and excel as a player and a teammate.

# HOMEWORK

The only homework assignment for chapter 6 is to carefully consider and list what you can do to be a better team player. Then do it and be it.

# CHAPTER
## 8

# Personality Differences

In the first seven chapters, I outlined some basic mental training principles and skills for playing winning hockey. Although these principles and techniques apply to almost everyone, people are different. In this chapter, we will discuss how players differ from each other and how these differences may affect preparation, dealing with pressure, and playing the game.

Players differ in many ways. For example, they differ in physical attributes such as size, strength, and speed, and they also differ psychologically in terms of attitude, experience, intelligence, and personality.

Personality differences exist among players and coaches. Our interest is in how these differences affect preparation and performance. In addition to the traits explored in the ASP test (discussed in chapter 6), some of the most relevant differences in personality style to consider are

- introversion vs. extroversion,
- task orientation (analytical, thinking) vs. feeling orientation (intuitive, social),
- type of focus (external, internal, broad, narrow),
- detail (specifics) orientation vs. general ("big picture") orientation, and
- vertical vs. horizontal thinking.

# INTROVERTS AND EXTROVERTS

Let's look at introversion–extroversion first. In chapter 4, I pointed out a direct relationship between the amount of emotional intensity or arousal a player experiences and the player's performance. With either too much or too little emotional intensity, performance is less than optimal. The relationship is depicted in figure 8.1.

The relationship between emotional arousal and performance can be complicated by a personality factor like introversion–extroversion. In general, introverts tend to be more sensitive and more affected by pressure. They overload more easily than extroverts. In contrast, extroverts tend to be more stimulus seeking and may require a higher level of arousal to be at their best. This relationship is depicted in figure 8.2.

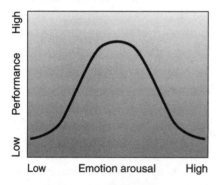

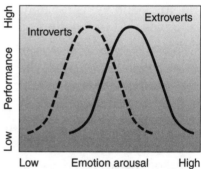

**Figure 8.1** Relationship between emotional arousal and athletic performance.

**Figure 8.2** Introverts and extroverts react differently to emotional stimuli.

In terms of pregame preparation, this can mean that introverts may play better if they learn ways to stay calm before a game. Introverts seem to function better with a clearly defined pregame routine to help them manage emotion. This reduces unnecessary last-minute surprises and limits rushing, both of which can be arousing and anxiety producing. Introverts prefer things to occur on time and take pride in having their equipment in order. This is a useful behavior.

A possible downside, however, is that introverts sometimes become preoccupied with the minor details and ritual of preparation and can upset themselves with small deviations in their pregame routine. To allay any potential anxiety, it can be useful to remind the more introverted player (or coach) to relax. Introverts can benefit from being reassured that they are prepared, things will be fine, and they can deal with any minor alteration in routine or schedule that may present itself. A pregame breathing session, positive self-talk, and mental rehearsal are all useful mental skills for an introverted player.

Extroverts may actually require stimulation, interaction, and a challenge to get into their optimal arousal zone. They may have difficulty organizing well in advance and often wait until the last minute to get going. This can lead to some last-minute confusion regarding equipment and scheduling their time. It's advisable to encourage extroverts to develop a pregame preparation routine that helps them do what's necessary to get themselves ready to play.

I recall Zeke, an extroverted team leader, talking trash in the bus on the way to a junior game. He expressed some of his anxiety by broadcasting critical comments about the team's effort in their last game, the previous day's practice, the pregame schedule, the timing in getting to the rink, and even the route the bus driver was taking to the game. When the team got into the dressing room and began to dress for the game, Zeke, who had been so busy with these other details, realized that he forgot to pack his skates.

Most players and coaches fall somewhere between the extremes of introversion and extroversion. You need to be aware of who you are and who your teammates are, and to respect the differences that exist between people. You deserve to exhibit your abilities, and so do they.

Of the many teams I have worked with, most have had a wide range of personality styles among players. Music preferences can reflect some of these differences. Music can be used to regulate emotional states. Before a game, some players like to listen to loud rock and pump up, some like heavy metal, others like Western or calming music, and some prefer quiet. Take note of what you like to do and listen to before a game in order to feel ready to play. Become more aware of the needs of others. Respecting these differences and having some flexibility is part of successful team preparation. Failure to attend to individual differences can cause player or team problems, even at the highest levels of competition.

Another distinction between introverts and extroverts is that the latter tend to be more social and outgoing. In getting up for a game, the extrovert is more apt to get energy from the competitive confrontation ahead of him—from the anticipation of "me or us against them." The introvert is more inner focused and may be more motivated by the personal challenge to execute well.

With regard to intrateam interaction, extroverts enjoy talking and joking with teammates before a game, even challenging them. Introverts, on the other hand, are more apt to prepare quietly. They often warm up and mentally rehearse aspects of their game by themselves. Joking around can be a disturbing distraction for them right before a game. I've observed players and coaches who were aggressive extroverts use stimulation and confrontation to get themselves and their teammates or players up before and during the game. On occasion, they will challenge their teammates to "show up." For some players, a direct in-your-face challenge can spark them to perform well. For others, it has the opposite effect.

I know of one player (we'll call him Jones) who was yelled at and sworn at so often by his coach in his first year in the NHL that his teammates gave him the nickname "F_____." When I asked one of his teammates why, he explained that every time the coach talked to or about Jones, he would say, "F____ Jones did this" or "F____ Jones can't do that." A dozen years later, after Jones had established himself as a very competent NHL player, I asked him about the story. "Yeah, it's true," he reflected. "And I want to tell you, it's no fun driving to work in the morning with your guts in a knot because you know the coach is going to yell and swear at you. It certainly didn't help me to play better. It was only later, when I was treated respectfully, that I became a better player."

I was talking to a bantam team about preparation. One player asked, "What's the best way to prepare?" I said, "Preparation is a personal thing. There are many elements that go into quality preparation. Rest, diet, practice, mental rehearsal, and power thinking are all important parts of preparing yourself to excel. It's important for you to discover what you need to do to be most effective."

The game-day preparation sheet (figure 8.3) provides a way of scheduling your time and managing your energy level from well before the game right up to and through the game. Thinking things through in advance may help you get a clearer mental picture of exactly what to do to prepare and play well.

Understanding who you are and what style works for you can be very helpful. One thing you can do to gain insight is to recall those times when you played your best. Think back and ask yourself, "What did I do to prepare on those high-performance days?"

# Game-Day Preparation

Name _____

Game _____ Date/time _____ Home/away _____

**Before Game**

Bedtime _____ Hours of sleep _____ Wake-up time _____

**Daily activity: Morning**

Breakfast food _____ Time _____

School or work _____ Pregame skate _____

Focus _____

Treatment/rehab, yes or no _____ If yes, what _____

_____

**Daily activity: Afternoon**

Lunch food _____ Time _____

School or work _____ Rest time _____ from _____ to _____

Relaxation/breathing _____ Hydration _____

Imagery/mental rehearsal _____

Self-talk _____

Dinner/snack food _____ Time _____

**Before leaving for the game**

Check equipment, telephone _____

Departure time _____ Ride _____ Arrive at rink time _____

**Pregame activity**

Check equipment (skates/sticks/pads) _____

Physical treatment _____

**Mental preparation**

Relaxation breathing _____

*(continued)*

**Figure 8.3** Use the game-day preparation sheet to schedule your time before, during, and after a game.

*(continued)*

Imagery/mental rehearsal (ABCs) _____

_____

Self-talk (power words and thoughts for the game) _____

_____

On-ice warm-up focus _____

In the room focus _____

**During game**

Things to do/remember _____

Work hard _____ Think positive _____ Hydrate _____

Power words _____

Between shifts, remember to _____

If there are long waits between shifts, remember to _____

Between periods, relax/recharge _____

Think positive _____

Hydrate _____

**After game**

Evaluate performance: 3 (excellent), 2 (average), 1 (poor)

Energy level _____ How legs felt _____ Mental sharpness _____

Pat yourself on the back. Things I did well and will continue to do well are:

_____

_____

_____

Things to improve and work on in practice are:

_____

_____

_____

**Figure 8.3** *(continued)*

## Best Performance

Go back and visualize a game in which you performed to the best of your ability. Fill out the game-day preparation form based on your activities that day. Then do the same for a game in which you played poorly. Compare the two. Note any significant differences. This may help you identify and develop some pregame behaviors or a pregame routine that works for you.

---

John Vanbeisbrouck, an NHL all-star goalie with 16 years of NHL playing experience, is one player I would describe as thoughtful and serious about his pregame preparation. He has his own specific game-day routine. He starts with a light breakfast. At the morning skate, he focuses on preparing himself. Sometimes he watches the other team's shooters, but never their goalies. He avoids interviews the day of the game. He has his main pregame meal at 12:30 P.M., usually a set menu of high carbs, chicken or fish, no spices. Following the meal, he relaxes and does some inspirational reading, then takes a nap. When he awakens, he watches TV (nothing serious) for about half an hour, then has a light snack. He gets to the rink early so that he has time to do some visualization and stretching before dressing.

During the game, he maintains his focus on the puck, even during stoppages in play. "My job is to stay focused on the puck, and that's what I do for the entire game. I don't skate over to the bench during stoppages in play. I don't think it's the time to socialize."

What John and more introverted goalies pride themselves on is their self-control and their ability to stay focused on the puck and not allow themselves to be distracted by anything, such as being bumped, screened, or by what happened in the last shift, the last period, or the last game. They think, "Nothing can distract me."

Contrast that with the style of goalies like Billy Smith, Patrick Roy, and Garth Snow, who are more extroverted and enjoy getting involved in the action. They have been known to mix it up with opposing forwards who invade the crease, crash the net, or come out to play the puck in dangerous situations. These extroverts, who seem to thrive on confrontation, have to remind themselves not to be too confrontational. The extroverted goalie must evaluate whether being confrontational actually helps or hinders his play. If being bumped bothers him and retaliating is a distraction

During a game, John Vanbeisbrouck didn't allow distractions to break his focus on the puck.

that gets him off his game, a goalie had better learn to manage his emotions and strengthen his focus.

I asked Billy Smith, the famed Islanders goalie, if a more extroverted, confrontational-style goalie needs to have more mental discipline to avoid becoming distracted and losing focus. Billy said that if you're going to play a more confrontational game, "Sure, you have to be smart and have discipline." Then he repeated a trademark line: "I never retaliated. I only initiated."

As for John, his pregame routine was something he developed over time, something that worked for him. My experience is that pregame routines vary considerably. Some players mentally rehearse their game in detail, whereas others prefer to deal with pregame pressures by distracting themselves. Some players have set routines like John; others are more casual and vary their pregame behavior. The important thing is to learn what works for you.

I often make audiotapes for players to use before games to relax and help them visualize. These tapes usually consist of a brief, five-minute section on relaxing and breathing and sending energy out through the body. Another five-minute section combines right feelings with mentally rehearsing playing good offense and defense. Not surprisingly, some players find the tapes more useful than others. I think tapes are most effective when they are personalized to address a player's style, the specific behaviors he wants to rehearse, and the emotional state he wants to achieve.

While working as a sport psychologist for the Los Angeles Kings, I made a generic pregame warm-up tape for all the forwards. It contained the "right feeling, right focus" formula that I discussed in chapters 2 through 6. About two weeks after I had given out the tapes, one of the players, an extrovert, asked if he could speak to me. When we met, he returned the tape, saying, "Thanks a lot for the tape, Dr. Miller, but it just doesn't seem to work for me. I play better when people give me s__." Although I didn't give him exactly what he asked for, I did make another tape for him that combined positive imagery with aggressive, challenging, confrontational comments.

## THINKERS AND FEELERS

Another personality style difference between players is that some are more thinking, analytical, and task oriented, whereas others are more feeling and people oriented. This style difference is a matter of perspective and how players prefer to be acknowledged. Feeling-oriented players are more social. They are concerned with how they feel, how others feel, and of course, how others see and feel about them. They tend to play with passion and respond to a pat on the back. They appreciate people acknowledging them for who they are (e.g., "You are a good player," "You're someone I can really count on"). They are often upset by others saying negative or uncomplimentary things about them.

Task-oriented players are primarily concerned with the elements of the task at hand—with analyzing what has to be done and doing it. They are less sensitive to general personal criticism and are more responsive to being acknowledged for a specific play or competency (e.g., "I liked the forecheck at the start of that shift, especially the way you went into the corner hard, pinned your man against the boards, and then got the puck"). Because of their task focus, at times these players may appear to be less emotional and less aware of or sensitive to the needs of other players on the team.

Players and coaches should be aware of these differences in perceptual style. They should recognize that some players focus more on performing the specific tasks required by their position and role on the team, whereas others are more tuned into the social aspects of participation in a team game. Again, you should understand who you are and have the flexibility and balance to express your style in preparation and training.

## DETAILERS AND GENERALIZERS

Another personality dimension that differentiates players is that some are more specific and detail oriented, whereas others are more big-picture generalizers. Are you a detailer or a generalizer?

Detail-oriented players highlight differences. They can be exacting, and they often focus on small imperfections. They enjoy creating and maintaining order. As part of their preparation, they often break down the performance of specific tasks ("If we are in their end with the puck, I do _____. If they are in our end with the puck, I do _____.") into elements, incorporating these elements into their mental rehearsal. They may consider in detail how they will perform each element. Sometimes they get too focused on detail and too upset by minor imperfections in their play. At those times, they should be encouraged to step back, take a breath, and look at the big picture—at what the team is trying to accomplish.

Generalizers see the big picture. They read the overall pattern of the game, but they tend to pass over or skip detail. If you are coaching a generalizer, remember that he might benefit by bringing a sharper, more detailed focus to his perspective and imagery. A good suggestion is for him to go back to those days when he really excelled and reflect on what he did to prepare and perform. The player should go through the pregame preparation sheets to see that they encompass everything he might do to prepare from the time he gets up—details such as what he has for breakfast and what he says to himself between periods and after the game. Players who are more introverted and those who are more task and detail oriented are more likely to approach this evaluation with some interest. Their reports are apt to be more thorough. It's more difficult to encourage extroverts to fill in these preparation sheets or to keep a training journal.

An elite youth team I worked with began journaling at the start of the season. Their coach asked them to write down their goals, any skills to be improved, and what and how they prepared for each game. He felt this process really helped his players be more focused, accountable, *response-able,* and effective.

Journaling means keeping a detailed record of how you prepare, train, and play. Although few hockey players seem to do it, journaling can be useful to the performance process. If you keep good journal notes, you can always go back and answer the question, "What did I do (or not do) on that day when I really played great?" You have a personal record of it. It is a kind of self-feedback/debriefing process.

# FOCUS

What's your focusing style? Another area of personality difference, and one that may correlate with introversion and extroversion, is focusing style.* Some players focus more on externals, and others focus more internally.

Externally focused players attend more to things around them (e.g., circumstances in the game, the rink, the crowd, their teammates). They may pay less attention to how they feel and what's going on inside them. Often they are not good at when and how to pump themselves up or calm down.

The flip side of the coin is those players who are more internally oriented. Although they may have a clear idea of how they feel, they may be less cognizant of what is going on in the game around them.

In addition, width of focus can vary from broad to narrow. Players with too broad an external focus may be easily distracted and may react to anything or everything going on around them. Players with a narrow internal focus have a tendency to become overly self-reflective and excessively focused on their anxieties, aches, and pains. Players' focusing styles can affect how they read the game, how they manage themselves, and their coachability.

---

*For information on focusing style, see the Test of Attentional and Interpersonal Style (TAIS) developed by Robert Nideffer and distributed by Enhanced Performance Systems.

# COACHING DIFFERENCES

Coaching provides an excellent opportunity and challenge to understand the marked range of personality differences that exist among players. Of course, the same differences that exist among players can also be found among coaches. Coaches can be introverted or extroverted, feeling or task oriented, detail people or generalizers, and internally or externally focused. An effective coach is one who knows his own predispositions and can understand and relate to athletes of all styles.

A coach's personality style can interact with a player's personality. For example, an extroverted coach may more readily understand the needs of an extroverted player—what makes him tick and how to fire him up. To be more effective, however, the extroverted coach must adjust an energized and sometimes in-your-face style to the more sensitive personality style of the introverted athlete. The Jones example I described earlier in this chapter illustrates the counterproductive nature of that kind of miscommunication.

An introverted coach is likely to have some of the same control preferences as the introverted athlete and may be challenged to display the necessary fire and flexibility in dealing with a more outgoing, spontaneous, extroverted athlete. An extroverted coach may appreciate an extroverted player's appetite for input, spontaneity, and even confrontation. At times, however, he may be challenged to impose the order and structure necessary for an extroverted athlete.

Similarly, the very analytic, task-oriented coach may have a greater understanding of and ability to communicate with task-oriented athletes and may find it more challenging to give encouraging emotional support to the feeling-type player. A coach who is more detail oriented may have to make the effort to be less detailed with players who are generalizers and yet help them appreciate the value of exactness in their preparation. Indeed, whenever there are personality style or communication differences between player and coach, both parties would be well advised to take a breath or two and exercise a little more patience and flexibility.

Whether you are a coach or a player, the ideal is to assess and adjust. Get in touch with who you are and learn how to create the feelings and thoughts that help you get into your optimal zone. Clearly, differing personality styles do this in different ways. And there are different ways to coach players to help them perform at their best.

Cliff Ronning, a veteran of the NHL wars and coaching styles, said, "If I were coaching, I would try to be aware that every player has his own mind. It's important to know your players. Some are more sensitive than others. It's important to work with each individual. For example, introverts and extroverts are different. Some players need to calm down; others need to pump up. As a coach, I would try to help my players learn what they need to know to be better."

Minnesota Wild forward Darby Hendrickson agrees. "You can't treat everyone the same. Players and circumstances are different. I think coaching is most effective when it has an awareness of those differences and a feel for what's needed in the moment."

A veteran NHL winger, bothered by his coach's yelling and swearing, remarked, "Does he really think calling us dumb f___ helps us to play better?" The hockey tough player is willing and able to adjust to coaching style.

## CHANGE AND EXPERIENCE

Another aspect of individual difference to consider relates to the concept of change. Just as a child evolves and matures through his experience of life, a hockey player evolves through his experience of competition and training. Techniques that may have been useful at one stage of preparation may be of less use or no longer useful at a later stage.

Things change. For a rookie, being called up to play in a big game or playing in the playoffs often leads to great excitement or even overarousal as he attempts to meet the challenge of performing at a new and greater level of competition. To manage the anxiety, a rookie could benefit from doing some relaxing and breathing, and possibly some mental rehearsal and positive self-talk, as preparation before the game. After the rookie has played for several years, his experience of the game may be very different. What was once very exciting may now be experienced as just another game. Instead of calming himself down, the same player may now actually have to focus on pumping himself up to get into his optimal zone.

# PRACTICAL AND THEORETICAL PLAYERS

Another distinction between players is whether they are the practical or theoretical type. The practical player tends to be interested in what to do and how to do it. The more theoretical player has a greater interest in why it should be done. The detailed analysis and explanation often presented in coaching sessions run by a theoretical coach may seem long and boring to the practical player.

One piece of advice for coaches (especially the more theoretical, analytic type) is to avoid providing too much analysis to players, especially immediately before a game. Overanalyzing can get everyone thinking too much and is a turn-off for the more practical player, the extrovert, the generalizer, and the more instinctive/feeling player.

In the early 1980s, I worked with two different head coaches on a successful NHL team. One was a good teacher and strategist, a nice guy, and an intelligent, theoretical coach. The other was also intelligent, but was a practical fellow who could be sarcastic and in your face. It fascinated me to watch various players react to these different coaching styles. One practical, tough-guy winger, an extrovert, found the teaching of the theoretical coach excessive and "demotivating." One introverted, analyzer-type defenseman found the same coaching excellent and played his best hockey for that coach. In contrast, the practical, tough-guy winger excelled for the practical, confrontational coach, whereas the young analyzer-type defenseman found him to be too callous and critical at times.

# THINKING STYLES

Still another area of personality difference has to do with thinking style. Are you a more lateral or a more vertical thinker? Some players think more vertically. They tend to be more ordered, follow instructions, and process one thing at a time. They do not like ambiguity or change. In contrast, more lateral-thinking players tend to be more adaptive. They are less order-bound and can read situations and adjust more easily. This is most relevant when it comes to adjusting to changing assignments and switching linemates or defensive partners.

Bob was a motivated, coachable, veteran NHL defenseman—a conscientious defender and good at rushing the puck. At the time I worked with him, he was struggling with his game on a team that was struggling to win. He called me because he felt uncomfortable and was playing with less confidence than usual. "Most of the time I do the right things to prepare, but I still feel unsure of myself out there and I have one of the worst plus/minuses on the team. I should be happy about all the ice I'm getting. They even have me on the power play. But things are changing so much, I never know who I'm playing with, and we always seem to be out of synch. I feel like I don't know who's going to do what out there."

I encouraged Bob to continue doing what he was doing to prepare (relaxation and mental rehearsal). Then I explained to his coach that Bob was a very vertical-thinking player. He performed at his best when things were consistent and structured. Bob was most effective when he knew who he was playing with and what his and their roles were. Under those circumstances, he was a very reliable, competent NHL defenseman. However, when there was little consistency and structure, he had trouble adjusting and performed at less than his best.

Adam was an experienced NHL winger who was being double shifted. He had two different assignments on two different lines. He was a grinder on a checking line and a setup man on a high-scoring line. He sought me out because he found the contrast confusing. "I don't know what my ABCs should be, and it's messing me up," he said.

Most players perform best with a clearly defined role and familiar partners and linemates. Some players are more vertical and bothered by changing circumstances, whereas others are more lateral and adaptive and can more easily adjust to playing any position on any line and be effective.

*There is no good or bad, or right or wrong personality style.* It is simply a matter of differences between people. Growing your understanding of these differences can help you be a more complete player or coach.

# BIG GUY EASY SYNDROME

The last personality style that I want to discuss is one I call the big guy easy syndrome. Not everyone is gifted with the same tools or body size. One thing I have observed is that some large players who were big at an early age and who used their size to be successful at the lower levels (bantam, midget, school, and even junior hockey) don't seem to have developed the work ethic of their smaller counterparts.

If you're small, the only way to succeed is to work hard and keep moving. If you're big, sometimes your size, not your effort, can get the job done. Consequently, what some big men consider to be appropriate work output may be much less than that of their smaller teammates, and some may be inclined to laziness.

The answer to helping these big guys increase their work output isn't simply to tell them to work harder. In some cases, they actually have to be put on a structured program and even have the appropriate level of effort modeled for them.

I have seen big guys in junior hockey and the NHL who just do their thing and then cruise. They don't seem to understand that they have to give more. I recall one NHL prospect who had been a big star throughout his junior career being surprised and annoyed that he hadn't made the NHL team at the end of training camp. "I worked harder this summer than I ever worked before," he complained, as if working hard should automatically have entitled him to the reward of playing in the NHL. The truth is, he was an easy player who needed to train harder and work harder on every shift. After training and playing a few games with the NHLers, he saw how hard everyone else was working and began to appreciate the need to work harder. But it wasn't easy for him to adjust because he had developed some lazy habits that had become part of his identity.

Indeed, several NHL coaches, including Scotty Bowman, have said that if a player completes his development without learning how to work hard and what it takes to be successful in the process, it can be difficult if not impossible for him to turn things around and become an effective, mentally tough player in the NHL.

In chapters 9, 10, and 11, we review the basics of feeling, focus, and attitude as they apply to three key performance areas: scoring, playing defense, and goaltending. In addition, each chapter contains observations and insights of experienced NHL players and coaches who are or were experts at scoring, playing defense, and tending goal. The diversity of their experiences and insights makes it clear that there is more than one way to prepare for and play the game. How you choose to prepare and play depends on who you are, your role on the team, and the specific challenges you face.

I recommend that you read the coaching advice in each of the chapters. Reflect on your game—on what you want to improve—

and take what you can use. Scorers can learn from studying what defensemen and goalies have to say about focus and mental preparation, as well as what other scorers have to say about the offensive game.

# HOMEWORK

## Assignment 1: Reflect on Your Personality Style

Are you more of an extrovert or an introvert?

Are you more of a thinking person or a feeling person?

Are you more of a task-oriented person or a generalizer?

Are you more internally or externally focused?

Are you more broad or narrow in focus?

Most people have elements of both extremes in their personalities. If one element is clearly dominant, then review the game preparation sheet and consider what adjustments you need to make in your game preparation to help you prepare better.

## Assignment 2: Game Preparation

Fill in the game preparation sheet for your next three or four games and review the input.

## Assignment 3: Skill Improvement

For the next month, before each practice, select a specific skill or conditioning element that you are going to work to improve that day. Before practice, write down what drills you might do to improve that ability. After practice, write down any observations you made during practice.

## Assignment 4 (Optional): Journal

Try keeping a journal for the next month.

# CHAPTER 9

# Scoring With an Offensive Mind-Set

In chapter 4, I presented a graph showing the relationship between emotional intensity and performance. If a player feels too tense, his performance may be negatively affected. Similarly, if a player is too laid back and not sufficiently intense, his performance may also suffer. I have seen both kinds of problems with scorers.

Most common is the scorer who feels tight and is trying too hard. He is squeezing the stick and forcing it. The best advice for him is to change feelings and focus. To do that, I recommend that the player release, breathe, and refocus. I emphasize breathing because it has helped many players manage their feelings effectively. Releasing and breathing can clear the mental TV screen of negative or high-pressure feelings and make it easier to focus on making the play and doing what you can to score or shut down your opponent. Players who report they play more on instinct often regain their touch just by releasing tension and tuning into right feelings.

Dan was more of a checker than a scorer, but he did generate scoring chances and wanted to be more effective at capitalizing on those chances when they were there for him. He felt he was always rushing himself around the net. He asked how he could develop the sense that he had more time. One suggestion was for him to focus on breathing, specifically on rhythm. We did some off-ice training in which Dan would focus on slow, smooth breathing, especially giving himself time for each breath to come all the way in and go all the way out. Then he would imagine (mentally rehearse) reacting smoothly, effectively, and with composure in a variety of scoring situations—getting a rebound in front of or around the net, holding the puck, waiting that extra half second for the opening, and scoring; making a short pass, then going hard to the net to take the pass and flick the puck into the net; circling into the slot, taking a pass, seeing the opening, and shooting accurately into the net.

When a scorer is tense and overaroused, I usually suggest that he relax, breathe, and practice creating smooth feelings (five-pointed star) and that he use affirmations such as "good hands" or "in control, with time." Imagery also can be useful for creating positive focus that can enhance scoring.

The imagery that is most beneficial is mental rehearsal. See yourself working your ABCs and having great finish: moving your feet, getting open, having a hard, accurate shot, being quick, being lucky, and putting the puck in the net. Stimulating images such as a panther or tiger hunting—being quick as a cat and strong in front of the net—can also help your scoring game.

Some players would score more if they played a more aggressive, attacking, go-for-it brand of hockey. Some lack confidence. Others are simply underaroused and need to get fired up.

Jim was an NHL winger, a big guy who was dangerous when he went hard to the net, but he rarely did. Occasionally he would get fired up—usually after a cross-check or a slash—and when the fire got lit, he could crash and score. Jim's problem was that he didn't know how to pump himself up, and it happened too infrequently. You need to know what feelings help you play your best and how to create those feelings.

Scoring has a lot to do with attitude. Many of the qualities of a winning attitude (discussed in chapter 5) come into play in scoring. You have to be *committed* to work on basics such as skating, passing, and shooting. You have to be *assertive* in going to the net and battling for position in front, even when the lumber is heavy. You have to be *confident*, to believe you can score, to go for it, and be a shooter.

Confidence is ephemeral. When a scorer's confidence is strong, he wants the puck and believes he can do something with it. When a scorer (even a veteran NHL scorer) hasn't scored in a few games, confidence often fades, and with it goes the edge. Without confidence, scorers don't seem to get to the right place at the right time. They don't seem to win the one-on-one battles, and they don't seem able to pull the trigger. Maybe it's confidence, or maybe it's self-image, but many scorers have an almost egocentric or selfish attitude of "I'm the guy, give it to me." They want the puck. They believe they can score. They expect good things to happen, and they do.

All kinds of players score goals. There is no single personality profile of a scorer. Extroverts score, and so do introverts. Task-oriented types and feeling types can both be scorers. Different adjustments can be made to help each of these types play and score effectively.

As a coach, you need to know when to confront, challenge, and provide more structure for an extrovert and to calm and encourage the more introverted type of scorer. Some helpful coaching strategies include watching tapes and analyzing play with the task-oriented scorer and taking the time to support the feeling player before or while offering advice.

Another difference is that some scorers are more analytical or left-brained. These players like to analyze and visualize what they have to do and then go out and do it. They find it helpful to review their ABCs and do mental rehearsal. Although the more instinctive or feeling right-brained players prefer not to think too much about things before games, working with ABCs and imagery can still be beneficial when used well in advance of a game.

Work hard. One tip that has helped many servers who are struggling is to contribute by focusing on other aspects of their game. Work harder on your defensive game, become a more aggressive checker, maintain excellent position, win the boards, move your feet, create good breakout opportunities. Generate chances and good things will follow.

# THE SCORER'S PERSPECTIVE

I asked a few veteran NHL players who had the gift for putting the puck in the net to offer some mental tips on scoring. Whenever possible, I've tried to put their words and advice into the framework we discussed in chapters 1 through 6.

# Cliff Ronning

Cliff Ronning is a scorer I've consulted with for eight seasons. At first, the critics said he was too small to play the game, but this NHL all-star has scored almost a point a game for more than 16 years. Some keys to Cliff's success are his on-ice intelligence and his commitment to physical and mental preparation. Here are some of Cliff's mental tips on scoring.

"Scoring is all to do with timing. It's about not being too quick or too slow. It's arriving at the right time and being in control. You don't want to get too far ahead of the play." An analytical thinker, Cliff said, "Focus is key. You have to be focused on the play. I mean really focused on the ice. Sometimes when I'm tuned in, I see the ice surface as a series of little squares or triangles [and the game as] a series of potential two-on-ones."

As Cliff describes it, scoring is a balance between being aggressive, being tuned in and focused, anticipating the play, and making things happen, yet still being in the moment and able to react. Cliff has found the idea of good hands, good wheels, and good eyes useful. His ABCs are as follows:

A. Be alert.

B. Make good passes tape to tape.

C. Jump up into the hole.

D. Want to receive the puck.

E. Be in control and aware of what's around you.

F. Be confident with the puck. Be confident enough to hang onto the puck for a split second longer and take an extra second to make the play. Many scorers have the ability to be calm under pressure and be comfortable holding the puck that extra half second, which increases their on-ice intelligence and scoring potential.

G. Shoot hard. If you want the puck to go in, visualize it going into the net. Don't just send a hoper at the net. Shoot with intention. Make it happen. See the holes.

Cliff said he doesn't even look at the goalie or know where he is. He just sees mesh. Remember, you have to shoot to score. Get the puck to the net.

# Pavel Bure

For more than a decade, Pavel Bure has been one of the most exciting scorers in the game. He says, "I always try to read the game and the flow of the puck. Anticipating a turnover and where the puck may go is critical to getting a good jump. For example, when a defenseman is about to shoot the puck, I see where he is shooting from and I anticipate where the puck will go. I want to know how it will come off the boards [so I can] move to that spot on the blue line with the shot. In hockey, you have to continuously read the game and react."

Pavel, "the Russian Rocket," is famous for his electrifying breakaways. I once asked him if he had a focus on breakaways. He laughed and said, "Yeah, it's to get away from the guy behind me." As for his focus regarding the net and where he's going to shoot, he said, "It's a feeling thing. I don't think about where I'm going to shoot. It's an automatic reaction between mind and body. It's just making a move I've practiced thousands of times."

I asked Pavel what advice he might have for a young player with good hands and good wheels who wants to develop his offensive potential. He thought for a moment and then said, "The only advice I have is pretty general: work hard."

When it comes to pregame preparation, Pavel said rest is a key element for him. When I asked if he did any specific mental preparation before games, he said, "No. To be honest, the less I think about the game, the better."

A teammate of Pavel's once described him as one of the most competitive guys he had ever played with, so I asked Pavel about self-talk and if there were any specific things he said to himself during the game. "What I say to myself most often during the game is 'Don't get frustrated.'" I asked him how he dealt with being held or slashed by an opposition player. Without hesitating, Pavel replied, "If I get slashed by someone, I slash him back, right away. Then I forget about it." It's not exactly the advice I offered when I discussed mental toughness (chapter 6), but I guess it works for Pavel.

# Alexander Mogilny

Alexander Mogilny is another very talented hockey player with practical intelligence who has scored more than 400 goals in the

NHL, including 76 one year with the Buffalo Sabres. I talked with Alex on several occasions about sport psychology in the Soviet hockey program. He said he really had no exposure to it over there. I also asked him the same question I asked Pavel: "If you were coaching a talented young hockey player, is there some advice you might be able to offer to help him become a better scorer?"

"No, I don't think so," Alex said. "I think it's just something you are born with. You either have it or you don't." I approached him with the same question on another occasion, and again he demurred. Finally, after I persisted, he said, "Okay, okay. The only thing I can say is, if you want to score, you have to shoot the puck. Shoot the puck at the net."

## Paul Kariya

Paul Kariya is an NHL all-star winger who has used intelligence, speed, and an excellent shot to become a prolific scorer. Here are his ABCs for scoring:

A. You have to shoot the puck to score.

B. Get your shot away quick and shoot on the net. Paul explained, "I'm not always trying to hit a specific spot. Sometimes I don't know exactly where a shot is going to go. I may be thinking of a spot. The goalie may even be sensing the same spot. The shot may not go exactly where I wanted it to, and still it beats him. To score, you've got to shoot the puck, shoot it quick and on net."

C. Get into good scoring position. "That might be the high slot for me or in front of the net for a power forward. You don't score many goals from the corner."

I asked Paul if there were specific things he said to himself during the game to stay focused. "I am a believer in positive, constructive thinking," he said. "But I don't like to think too much during the game. It's important to be in the moment. As Yogi Berra said, 'How can you think and hit at the same time?' Sometimes during the game I may remind myself to get my focus back. Or if something upsets me, I'll tell myself to park it. But I believe a key to performing well is not to think too much and to stay in the moment."

## Steve Yzerman

Steve Yzerman, a great all-around team player and scorer, agrees that attitude and shooting ability are keys to scoring. "A lot of it is attitude. It's having pretty good nerve in front of the net or on a breakaway and being able to wait the goalie out. It's hard to explain, but goal scorers have confidence. They believe they're going to get the puck in the net."

Regarding pregame preparation, Steve echoed Pavel's and Paul's comments about resting and trying not to think too much about the game before playing. He said, "I take the opposite approach of a lot of guys who try to get fired up. Early in my career, I didn't want to talk to anyone. It was all hockey, from the night before the game right up to game time—a real serious approach. But I couldn't maintain that over my career. For the last few years, my approach has been to do everything I can to take my mind off the game. If I'm coming to a crucial game or in the playoffs, I know I'll be ready when the game starts. I don't need to get psyched up."

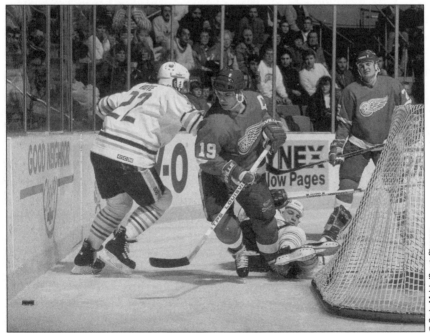

© Craig Melvin/SportsChrome

Steve Yzerman stays focused and calm and doesn't allow distractions to break his concentration on the puck.

Steve continued, "The best thing you can do is relax and take it easy. You'll be more energetic, as opposed to getting yourself all fired up, coming out on the first shift at 100 miles per hour, and it's all downhill from there. Being relaxed, you conserve a lot more energy and your skills take over, and you rise to the importance of the situation instead of trying to build yourself up to it."

Regarding dealing with frustration, Steve says, "I try to stay calm. Once you get rattled and distracted, it takes away from what you're trying to do. The more you can stay calm and not get distracted by someone or something else, the better off you're going to be."

I asked Steve what a young player could do to develop his scoring ability. Along with lots of practice and hard work, he suggested, "It's important to work on your shot . . . with your head up . . . seeing where you're shooting the puck and not just blasting it straight into the goalie's pads."

Steve also said it's a good idea to study goalies' tendencies and how they can be scored on. "A lot of these guys are flopping down now and putting their sticks on the ice. You never used to be able to score high on the blocker side, but now you can because they drop a shoulder as they lower the stick. That's where you've got to shoot. Now you don't have the five-hole, but you have that spot high on the blocker side. So studying the styles of goalies helps, but mostly it's shooting the puck." Steve added, "After practice we like to fool around doing mini breakaway drills. We're always trying to score, always trying to put the puck in the net."

## Mark Messier

Mark Messier is another remarkable team leader and scorer. When I asked Mark about scoring, he told me, "I'm not the right guy to ask about scoring goals." I protested that since he was the second-highest scoring center of all time, having netted more than 600 NHL regular-season goals plus another 100 in the playoffs and more than 2,000 points, he was more than qualified to speak on scoring.

"Well," he replied, "my focus has never just been scoring. It's been winning and doing whatever had to be done to win. There's a difference. Had I been a pure scorer, someone like Mike Bossy, I may have been able to score more goals. But I varied what I did depending on the needs of the team. Sometimes it was scoring, sometimes it was playing a more defensive role, and sometimes it was being more of a team leader." Clearly, there's a difference between being a pure scorer and an all-around team player.

Wayne Gretzky confirmed what his former teammate said and offered this assessment of Mark's motivation and focus: "The measure of Mark's game is not in goals and assists. The statistic he cares about is the number of Stanley Cups won" (Gretzky 1996).

Mark shared some observations on scoring. "I think one of the biggest areas of change in hockey over the last 20 years has been goaltending. The equipment is better and goalies are better technically. I think it's harder to score. It used to be that when you would skate down the wing, the goalie would play tight on the near post and not come out or cut off the angle. You could actually see space between the goalie and the far post, and if you made that shot, you would score."

"But you still score from the wing," I told him, then asked about his patented wrist shot, which he takes off his back foot as he's coming down the wing. "Why is that shot so effective?"

"I come down the wing with speed, and just before I shoot, I move laterally as well as toward the net. That causes the goalie to adjust. Sometimes I am able to catch the goalie moving. When I can do that, there are some openings and he can be beaten."

Mark expressed some definite views about the importance of preparation that relate to every phase of the game, including scoring. "Preparation begins well before a player gets to the rink the night of a game," he says. "Over the summer months before the season starts, you build strength. Today in professional sport, with so many games and so much travel, you really have to learn how to build strength and stay in great shape to be effective. Every team has experts with good strength and conditioning programs. Some players follow them. How you feel affects how you think and play. When you are weak and tired, you feel more vulnerable and less confident. When you are strong, you feel more confident and more like you can make a difference.

"Game preparation should begin before you get to the rink. A lot of things go into it—thinking about the game, watching what other teams and other players do, and seeing what you can learn from that. Getting the right amount of rest, eating right, and having positive self-talk are all important parts of preparation. A lot of players don't know anything about self-talk. They don't realize that saying negative things to themselves, even when they are not playing, can lead to more negative play.

"It's important for a team to have some time just before the game to bring their energy together. After team meetings [and after the players have spent] some time in the training room and adjusting equipment, I like to see everybody in the room with the music off an hour before game time. That time together is special. It doesn't always have to be the guys talking about the game. Sometimes there's humor. But it's the guys talking together and coming together as a team. That's very important."

## Luc Robitaille

Luc Robitaille can score. Indeed, he did so frequently, he's been nicknamed "Lucky." Over 15 NHL seasons, Luc has scored more than 600 goals. I met Luc in his first year in the NHL when I was a sport psychologist with the Los Angeles Kings. He's a nice guy, and it's been a pleasure to observe his evolution into one of the league's top scorers.

Luc is an instinctive/feeling-type player, and he generously shares his ideas about focus and preparation. "After a shift, I never think back on things I missed on the ice," he says. "That's past. Instead, I focus on what's happening now. I see where people are getting open. I see where the puck should go. It's important to watch and be aware."

Luc went on to say, "When I played with Gretzky, I noticed he watched everything. He was very aware. He could tell you who scored and assisted on all the goals. And if a player was injured, Wayne was the first guy on the ice to replace him. Of course, the more you play, the more you pick up. I watch the other guys to see what I can learn."

About preparation, Luc says, "Work hard in practice. Practice the system. You must know where you should be on the ice. [Know your ABCs.] And you must work out, have good nutrition, and rest."

Beyond that, Luc says to do whatever works. Do what feels comfortable to you. "Everybody has their own way to get ready. The easier you make it for yourself, the better. Some players are too inflexible about their preparation routine. I'm not. Before the game, we get information about the other teams on paper. I look it over, but I don't like to worry too much about it. I really like to be at ease with my mind. The less I think about the game, the better off I am. I produce on instinct. I find when I think too much about what I should be doing, I get behind."

When it comes to visualization, Luc says, "I do some visualization from time to time. However, I find when I visualize myself scoring, I think about it too much and it slows me down." He continues, "Hockey is different from other sports. It's different from basketball, football, and golf. There are no set plays in hockey. There are no free throws or patterns that you can visualize exactly as they'll take place. Hockey is all reaction. Everything happens because of someone else's mistakes. You have to be able to react. You have to be creative to score."

I mentioned to Luc that many players use some form of visualization. "I think visualization is more useful for a defensive player," Luc says. "Defense is more of a set game. They are playing more of a system and more one-on-one. But to put the puck in the net you must be creative." Clearly, Luc knows what works for him. Of course, mentally rehearsing taking a pass and beating the goalie can be effective preparation. Remember the concept of scoring 50 goals a day. It works.

I asked Luc what advice he would have for a youngster with good skills that might help him become a better player and a better scorer. "I would teach him the basics of the game. Then I would watch and see if he practices them and whether he is willing to work hard. I would decide whether he really loves to play hockey or not. People can help, but it's got to be up to you." Like Pavel Bure and Mark Messier, Luc believes that to be successful, you've got to work hard and love the game. If you do, you might get lucky.

## Markus Naslund

Markus Naslund has evolved into one of the NHL's top scorers. Like his colleagues, Markus underscores the importance of attitude, specifically confidence, in scoring. Markus says, "I take it one game at a time. When I'm playing well, I feel like I can score and I don't want to pass up a shooting opportunity."

Markus is an intense, serious athlete. He says, "It's important not to let negative thoughts phase you. I let them wash away before I come to play."

When I asked Markus about his ABCs, he listed the following:

A. Move your feet. "It's tough playing hockey standing still. I like taking the puck with speed."

B. Shoot the puck to score. You have to get your shots through.

When I asked him how he developed his accurate wrist shot, he replied that accuracy developed by playing and shooting a lot. "I never took target practice, but I would practice shooting into the open net, shooting just inside the post, shooting a great deal."

## WHAT MAKES A SCORER?

I spoke with a lot of shooters about scoring. I also thought goalies might have a unique perspective about what leads to scoring goals. I asked Mike Dunham, a veteran NHL and Olympic goalie, for any advice that might enhance a player's ability to score. Mike smiled and replied that he didn't want to give away any trade secrets. Then he added, "If you want to score, shoot the puck. Shoot it from any angle. When you shoot the puck, anything can happen. The goalie can be screened, there can be a deflection, a tip-in, a rebound. If you want to increase your scoring, my advice is shoot the puck."

There are many theories as to what made Wayne Gretzky a great scorer. Some people say it was his ability to see the ice, anticipate, read patterns, and innovate. Others point to his remarkable stick skills and aerobic capacity. When Gretzky was at his best, Rick Lanz, a young NHL defenseman, commented on Gretzky's remarkable ability to hold the puck: "He makes me make the first move." Rick, now a veteran coach, and I were discussing scoring recently, and he made another point: "People like Gretzky, Kariya, Naslund, and Ronning are very comfortable on their skates. Moving on ice is second nature to them, and consequently they are free to concentrate totally on puck movement. Many other players focus on just getting there. Gretzky's focus was entirely on the play."

A key question, of course, is whether this ability to be cool under pressure, to hold the puck that extra half second and then to execute effectively, can be taught. I believe it can, at least to some extent. I've come up with six training areas that I think could improve a player's ability to be calm under pressure and execute well.

1. The player must improve his skating ability so that skating becomes second nature and one less thing to think about. This frees him to focus more on the puck.

2. The player has to develop a scoring focus so he's positive and aggressive about taking the puck to the net and shooting it.

As all scorers stressed, shoot the puck. You've got to shoot to score.

3. The player has to work on managing his emotions so that he can attack offensively, hunt pucks and battle in front of the net, and remain calm under pressure. That involves breathing, releasing, and being a star, techniques we discussed at length in chapter 4.

4. Although some of the scorers said they didn't do visualization before a game, I can't stress enough the importance of doing some mental rehearsal. I believe it can be useful to visualize shooting and scoring. Imagine being calm, handling the puck, making and receiving passes, and finishing.

5. Learn to read patterns of puck flow so that, like Bure or Gretzky, you can anticipate where the puck is going and be one step ahead. The earlier a player learns to read the game, the more profoundly it can influence his development. Psychologists have observed that early experience shapes later learning, in some cases even influencing neuroanatomy.

6. It's essential to combine imagery with actual on-ice practice to improve stick skills, passing, shooting, and puck handling, as well as reinforce keeping your head up so you can see what's happening rather than looking down at the puck. By practicing your stick skills and developing your shot and your goal-scoring reflex, you will maximize the scoring opportunities you generate with hard work.

When I ask players to capsulize their advice about scoring, the most consistent response I get is

A. Work hard.
B. Move your feet.
C. Shoot the puck.

Scoring is the result of doing the basics well and maintaining a positive mind-set. Instead of worrying about the end result, work on the basics. Do the mental and physical training. Create right focus and right feelings. See yourself performing well. Remember, confidence comes from preparation as well as from success.

# CHAPTER 10

# ⌐Defending and⌐
# ⌐Checking Tough⌐

Playing good defense involves the same basics of right focus and right feelings described in chapters 1 through 7. The only difference is that some people believe defense may be the most difficult position to play in hockey.

Playing good defense requires a diversity of skills. A defenseman has to have game smarts, strength, mobility, and reliable hands. Defensemen have more responsibilities and must make more consequential reads than forwards. Defensemen must have more mobility and be physically stronger than goalies. If a defenseman fails to tie up a 220-pound center in front of the net or gets beaten one-on-one by a speedy winger, the consequences can be embarrassing and costly, all of which means the position is a greater challenge to play. It's not surprising, therefore, that defensemen mature more slowly than forwards—indeed, many NHL defensemen are not truly comfortable and confident playing their position until they are in their mid- to late 20s.

The ABCs to playing defense effectively are

A. good eyes,

B. good wheels, and

C. good hands.

As I mentioned, strength also helps.

Good eyes means good vision, especially good peripheral vision. One point that every defenseman I spoke with articulated is the need to make good reads. By that they mean being aware of who is on the ice, where they are, what is happening and anticipating what could happen next. Playing good defense when the other team has the puck is about anticipating their play and maintaining good position. Playing good defense when your team has the puck requires you to be aware of when and where to move the puck, and when to jump into the play, and to do it all quickly and with confidence. Awareness and timing are critical, both in reading opportunities and reacting at the right instant, whether it's gapping up properly (judging and matching your speed to the forward's speed) or stepping up and supporting the rush.

Bret Hedican, a speedy defenseman with the Carolina Hurricanes, says, "The speed of the play in the NHL is so fast that you have to know who's on the ice and where they are so you can anticipate and react almost before things happen." Bret went on to say that one of the real challenges for the young defenseman is to know what's going on and have the discipline to keep from just reacting and chasing the puck.

© SportsChrome

Good eyes are vital to good defense.

Kimmo Timonen is an NHL all-star defenseman who's proof that you don't have to be big to be good. This Finnish star is small by North American standards. When asked how he is able to deal with the bigger attackers in the physical North American game, Kimmo says, "It's really a matter of anticipation and good position. These are two keys to playing good defense. You have to know who's on the ice and anticipate what they may do, and you have to maintain good position. I don't try to muscle the bigger players. I use quickness and my ability to read the play to take away their game."

Larry Robinson, a perennial NHL all-star who twice won the Norris Trophy as the NHL's premier blue-liner, offers similar advice on the importance of being aware of what's happening around you. "A lot of kids are mesmerized by the puck," Larry says. "You have to look and read so you won't be surprised. Be aware. It's very important for a defenseman to know what to do before getting the puck. Know what's happening. Know who's coming at you. Know if you have time. Communication is also important. Talk out loud. If I was the guy carrying the puck, I might communicate to move a player. If someone were about to hit one of our players, I'd tell him to look out. I also used to talk to myself on the ice, just to keep myself focused."

Mark Hardy, a veteran of 19 pro seasons who is now a coach for the Los Angeles Kings, concurs. "For me, the most important things in playing defense were being in control and being consistent. I wanted to control my intensity and stay focused on doing the four or five basic things that I knew I had to do well."

Good wheels, like good eyes, are an asset to all players. For a defenseman, good wheels are fundamental to reading and reacting to the play. Superior skating ability can allow you to make things happen and to recover if you are caught in the wrong position.

Mattias Ohlund, one of the NHL's most reliable defensemen, explained that if a defenseman isn't skating well and is slow to the puck, he has less time to read the play and less opportunity to make good decisions. Defensemen who labor with their skating frequently find themselves struggling to catch up to the play and under pressure to react. Often they are forced to move the puck without a heads-up read of the situation.

If you are an aggressive forward, be aware that pressuring the forecheck means that the defense has less time to break out and start the rush. That usually leads to poorer decision making and generates more mistakes, especially for less mobile and less composed defensemen.

Good hands are a gift for a forward, but they're a must for a defenseman. Mishandling the puck in your end can be a disaster. Sure hands on defense reduce everybody's anxiety. By good hands I mean owning or protecting the puck, being able to take and make a pass, and controlling the puck at the point. A hard, accurate point shot is desirable, but remember, accuracy, which is the ultimate result of good control, is more important than just shooting hard.

Essentially, there are two styles of playing defense. D1 is the classic, stay-at-home defenseman. D1 tends to be a more physical player and is able to control or clear the front of the net and move the puck forward. His core game is his solid, reliable play in the defensive zone.

D2 has more of an offensive or rushing capability. In addition to playing good defense (the focus is always defense first!), D2 can make quick decisions about when to jump up into the play and has the wheels, eyes, and hands to make something happen on offense.

The distinction is important because responsibilities and mental preparation can be quite different for D1 and D2. For example, D1 sees himself as the bear or the lion. His mental rehearsal might encompass being strong and positionally sound, putting himself between the opponent and the goal he is defending, blocking shots, covering one-on-one and two-on-two situations, and clearing the territory in front of his net. In his mental rehearsal, he can see himself being unbeatable, handling the big forwards. When D1 closes on his opponents, they don't escape him. When he takes opponents to the boards, they're pinned.

D2 is more mobile. He views himself as the jaguar or the tiger. D2's mental rehearsal includes playing good positional defense, but it also features stepping up into the play, rushing the puck, moving to elude a checker, keeping the head up, passing the puck and receiving it, moving in back door, being strong at the point, having a good, accurate one-time shot on net, and scoring.

*How do you develop skilled defensemen?* I asked Pat Quinn, a former veteran NHL rearguard and a master coach. Pat said, "Good defense starts with learning the fundamentals. First, it's learning to play without the puck. It's learning to play your angles, to position yourself on the inside, to be able to put or move the attack where you want it to come, to play outnumbered, and to protect the goaltender."

Ken Hitchcock, a Stanley Cup-winning coach, agrees. "The single most important lesson that any defender can learn is that he doesn't need to have the puck to dictate what will happen. Learn how to invite the puck carrier to do what you want. Soon it will be on his [the defender's] stick" (Rossiter and Carson 1998).

Quinn also explained how when coaching a young, inexperienced defensive corps at the NHL or senior level, a coach may initially want to adopt a defensive style (such as a 1-2-2 trap) that protects the defensemen. In a system like that, the defense doesn't have to face the initial brunt of the attack. However, Pat cautioned, "There's a downside to playing in a defensive system all the time. If you do, you will blunt the maximum growth of the player. That's because this kind of defensive model never builds the offensive side of the player. You may win games 1-0, but the defensemen in this system will always be looking to make the safe play. They'll simply get rid of the puck, dump it out. The result of an overemphasis on this system is that the defensemen can't find the breakout pass and they can't create the rush. They don't learn the transition game, and they may never evolve to their offensive potential."

Pat was critical of young players being stuck in a system. "Until a player has developed to a reasoning stage, to a point where he can read and understand the game, he shouldn't be stuck in a system. Otherwise he will become too dependent on the system, and his perception, thinking, and offensive skills will be limited. Defensive systems work, but they just shouldn't be imposed upon young players too early."

At the higher levels, two challenges in playing defense are size and speed. I asked several NHL defensemen how they adjusted their game to play against size and speed. Bret Hedican says, "Playing against size, you may be up against players bigger than yourself. You can't just run at them and knock them down (unless they're off balance)." Like Kimmo Timonen, Brett says, "What's essential is to have good position. My focus is always be between them and the net."

Brett continued, "You also have to maintain good position against speed. Here anticipation is very important. Many of the speed players like Pavel Bure play on the edge, anticipating the turnover. They are breaking to the gap as the puck changes hands.

You have to be aware of that and be disciplined to know where they are and adjust accordingly." Bret's ABCs for playing against players with size and speed could be

A. good awareness,

B. good position, and

C. good wheels.

Gary Galley offers the following suggestions, drawn from his 17 years of experience as an NHL blue-liner. On defending against size, Gary says, "Don't give up space in the neutral zone. Big guys need space to get going; you can't let them get going. Give them space in the corners. Don't run them. Give them a yard and a half, then take it away. Look for their stick in front of the net. If you can't move the body, take the stick away and dish out little jabs on the back to distract them and prevent them from getting set."

I worked with Gary during his first year in the NHL with the Los Angeles Kings. He went on to play for Boston, Buffalo, Philadelphia, the Kings again, and then the New York Islanders. Along the way, he picked up a great deal of experience and some insights on focus, emotional control, and preparation. Gary says the key to playing good defense is to "be in charge." His ABCs were to

A. play good angles,

B. maintain good position, and

C. know who's on the ice at all times.

"The games when I really played well were the games when I was alert and in control," Gary says. "I think when you turn the corner and become a real NHL player, you'll find you know the players in the league, you know the danger areas, and you can control time and space. [In the process] you spend less time and energy in your zone chasing the man or the puck. Do your work in the neutral zone. Stand up. Turn pucks over. Work hard."

To prepare for a game, Gary likes to relax and run over things in his mind before going to the arena. In the dressing room before the game, he'll look over the other team's lineup and think about the opponent's tendencies. "I also find that sharing my thoughts with the younger players helps me to prepare. Usually, I don't know 10 to 15 percent of players on the other team, so I talk to others in the room about those guys. There are also things I say to myself—strategy thoughts about what to do in certain situations, control thoughts such as 'be poised' and 'be in control in any situation.' [That's important because] younger players feed off the composure of veterans. And I think about creating energy on the ice surface and having confidence with the puck. Consistency is also important. I want to be there and do these things every night. Of course, not every game is an oil painting, but to play good defense you must be in control, consistent, and able to adapt. When I'm not feeling in control, I take a few deep breaths. I try to stay positive and turn the negatives around."

Gary also repeated something that several other players have said: "Many coaches are simply too focused on the negative. You have to let the little things go. Some players don't take criticism very well. I'd say the large majority of players don't know how to use criticism and turn negatives into positives." That's an interesting observation. Turning negatives into positives is an important part of managing the mind. Remember, winners use everything.

Throughout his long career, Gary said he never stopped learning. "For me, it was a learning experience every time I stepped out onto the ice. Even in the pregame morning skate, I'd skate around playing pucks off the boards and the glass and trying to get to know the rink, the angles, and the bounces. It may have looked weird to someone else, but there's always more to know."

Chris Pronger, winner of the Norris (best defenseman) and Hart (most valuable player) Trophies, acknowledges that positioning is a huge part of the game. He says that great players seem to have a knack for being in the right place at the right time. They can read and react to the puck. If you are going to defend against them, you have to be in the right place mentally and physically. Chris uses visualization as part of his pregame preparation; however, he doesn't tailor his mental rehearsal to the specific team he may be facing that night. Instead, he runs through some positive imagery that prepares him to play against all teams.

I asked Jack McIlhargey, a Vancouver Canucks coach, what mental techniques he used to prepare for games in his 11 years as a player in the NHL. Jack said part of his preparation involved using both positive imagery and self-talk to get ready. He would tell himself that he was going to play a good game, and then he would imagine doing it. "Before every game I would go over the lineup of the team we were going to play and visualize their players, especially the most dangerous ones. I would see them coming in on me, visualize some of their better moves, and see myself playing the body, taking them out of the play, getting the puck, and moving it up, making a good, quick pass."

Jack believes the most important part of playing good defense is maintaining good position. "I always saw myself positioned between the opposing player and our goal." Jack added that another part of preparation is to keep your head in the game while sitting on the bench. "On the bench between shifts, I would watch the way the opposition forwards moved the puck and think how I would react in each situation. That way, my head was in the game and I was ready to play when my turn came up."

Larry Robinson agrees. "Too many guys come off the ice and dwell on what they did out there, especially what didn't go well. I don't think there's enough focusing on the positive aspect of the game. On the bench, it's important to be in the game, watch what the other team is doing, and know what you would do."

When he played, Larry says he didn't really use visualization in a systematic way to prepare for games. Instead, he would rest before games and keep his mind off hockey. "I found that thinking about the game made me too wound up. Especially the games [the Montreal Canadiens played] against the [Quebec] Nordiques. There was so much emotion and pressure to win those games. I would get too nervous. The most important thing in the game is reaction. I felt I played better when I didn't think too much about the game." Larry agrees with Luc Robitaille and Steve Yzerman when he says that hockey is different from sports like football, baseball, and golf in that there are no set plays and most of the game is instinctive. "You've got to react right now. I believe that if a player thinks too much or if a player has to pause and think about it, he will be late on every play."

Some say that the worst thing you can do in hockey is think. Obviously, that's a ridiculous overstatement. A hockey player has to know his job and what to do in every zone on the ice. He has to be able to read a situation, make good decisions, and react. All that involves thinking. Thinking is also the basis of mental preparation, which enables a player to anticipate and react instantly and appropriately. What should be avoided are uncertainty, indecision, and thinking too much. You don't want to be out on the ice trying to decide, "Should I do this or should I do that?"

Thinking is vital to hockey success. How you manage your thinking is up to you. Some players have found it very helpful to run through game situations in their mind immediately before a game to sharpen their anticipation and confidence. Others have reported that repeating power thoughts before a game and even between shifts helps them be more focused and positive. Some players who feel confident that they know their jobs find it most beneficial to simply relax before a game. Your style of preparation is a personal decision, but understand that the game's best players are smart players, and playing smart involves thinking.

Adrian Aucoin is a versatile and durable NHL defenseman and also a power-play expert. One tip he offers to improve power-play effectiveness is to study the most skilled players when their team has the advantage. "You can learn a great deal by watching other players like Al MacInnis quarterback the power play."

Adrian also has some advice about shooting from the point. "When you are playing the point on power plays, you want to get the puck to the net, and you want to avoid shooting into the shin pads of the checking winger. That can result in a short-handed goal for the other team. There's no one way of shooting from the point. You vary your shooting depending on the situation. For example, if the checker is high and on me quickly, my focus is to shoot to miss his shin pads or his stick by two inches in the general direction of the goal. When you have more time and can see the net, then you can pick your spots." Adrian said that he takes a half rather than a full swing. "It gives me a quicker release, especially when I'm shooting off a cross-ice pass and I can catch the goalie moving. If the goalie is set and square, I may try and drive it hard through him."

Andy Delmore is another NHL power-play specialist with an excellent point shot. He concurs with much of what Adrian has said. Andy's ABCs for shooting from the point are as follows:

A. Shoot to miss the skates and shin pads of the checker coming at you.

B. You don't have to shoot hard—you can take a half slap shot or wrist shot.

C. Shoot on net.

When I asked Ed Jovanovski for some tips on playing good defense, he said, "The biggest things for a defenseman are *position* and *patience* and *poise*." Ed's comment brings us back to two basics we discussed at the beginning of the book, namely, right focus and right feeling. Maintaining good position is about focus and making good reads. Patience and poise are feeling states and reflect emotional control. On poise, Ed said, "You've got to learn to relax. You just can't play well if you're uptight."

# CHECKING

Checking isn't the same as playing defense, but it is an important aspect of the defensive game. Although defensemen essentially defend the area between the opponent's blue line all the way back to their goal, the checker does much of his defending in the opponent's end and in the neutral zone.

The checker's role is to shut down the other team's scoring line, to stop their scorers from moving the puck and going to the goal. A good checker usually plays without the puck more often and for longer periods than he spends with it. It's a game of making reads and working hard, doing whatever is necessary to shut down the opposition.

The ABCs of most checkers would include things like the following:

A. Skate, skate, skate—go in hard and come back hard.

B. Make the right reads.

C. Maintain good position, play good angles, contain, and take the body.

Dave "Tiger" Williams was a tenacious checking left-winger in his NHL days. When I asked him about checking, he told me to talk to Bob Gainey. Bob is a model of hockey toughness. During his 16 seasons with the Montreal Canadiens, he set the standard for checking forwards, winning the Frank J. Selke Trophy (best defensive forward) four years in a row. He transformed checking from a trade into a craft, and as a coach and general manager with the Dallas Stars, he has helped develop some of the NHL's best checkers.

"From a mental outlook," Bob says, "a checker is a player who finds value in being a difficult opponent." Bob explained that a checker is unlike many players who only concern themselves with what they produce. The ledger of how a checker plays is not just measured in points. A good, solid checker relies primarily on two tools: his skating and his intelligence. "A good checker has the ability to get inside his opponent's head. He knows what he will try to do and what he can and can't accomplish. He knows when he needs to go there and when he doesn't, like when the opponent will mess the play up by himself. The really good checker is a two-way player. He's someone who is interested in the puck." He added, "Some players aren't. They take it and then they'll give it right back."

Bob underscored the importance of positioning in being a proficient checker. "Being effective is understanding and anticipating where the puck will go next and then getting there. You know, checking is a little like shooting pool. If you are in good position, there's never a hard shot."

When it comes to checking, Tiger Williams echoed the same sentiments about positioning as Hedican, Timonen, McIlhargey, and Quinn: "Always be between your opponent and your net. It's a must for playing good defensive hockey" (Williams and Lawton 1984). Tiger went on to say that it's mentally tougher to be a good checker than it is to be a scorer. Mentally, it's a bigger challenge night in and night out. "A good checker has to talk himself into doing a lousy job, one that's usually unacknowledged, and doing it well. It's often a thankless job. You can check the top snipers off the score sheet, but when it comes to negotiating next year's salary, they look at who scored 30 or 40 goals, and your efforts as a checker are often forgotten."

What sort of mind-set does it take to be a successful checker? "Be tenacious," Tiger says, "no matter what the score. You want the guy you're checking to be thinking to himself, 'Oh no, not this [guy] again. I hope he's not out there again.' When he starts to think 'Let's wait 'til next game when I don't have to deal with him,' your job as a checker defending him will be much easier."

When Tiger played in the league, many players felt exactly that way about him. I remember sitting in the dressing room with the Los Angeles Kings listening to players and coaches discussing strategies for how they dealt with Tiger being on the ice. Tiger went on to say, "It's during the playoffs that you really find out who the good checkers are because they have to face the same sniper for five or six games in a row. It's important for the coach to be committed to you and the matchup because if he switches you off an assignment, then the sniper can get the psychological edge."

Brad May, another hard-checking NHL winger, agreed with Tiger about checking and playoff hockey. "There's way more pressure in the playoffs," Brad says. "It's really a challenge to check the best and not just shut them down, but also to beat them." So how does he go about it? "You've got to be smart. You have to be intense and in the moment, but you also have to be in control and balance attacking with an awareness of time and position. Position is key to checking."

The evening before that conversation, I watched Brad battling for a playoff berth. Late in a close game, Brad provoked a St. Louis Blues player, who retaliated and got a penalty. Brad skated away. He agreed that it's hard to skate away from a confrontation and not retaliate, but in crucial situations and the playoffs, you have to play hockey tough—hard, smart, and with control.

Brad says checkers have to develop a unique mind-set. Once the coach tells you your role, that is all you should think about. "Even when you are sore and beat up, you must gear yourself up and lay it all on the line. I love the intensity. I love the playoffs."

Dave Scatchard of the New York Islanders is a 20-goal scorer who is often asked to play a checking role. According to him, these are the ABCs of checking:

A. Anticipate. Read the play and be one step ahead of it.

B. Good position is key. Put yourself between the opposition player and your goal.

C. Communicate with the defense. "Before every face-off I always make sure we know who's got who. When necessary, we switch."

Like everyone I asked, Dave stressed the importance of good reads and good position in being an effective checker. "Guys aren't going to be scoring from the corner. Position yourself so they have to go through you to get to the net."

Checking forwards, like defensemen, often have to deal with playing against scorers with greater size and speed. "When you are playing against good players, you've got to have good body position," Dave says. "Against big players, you absolutely have to be in the right place: there's no cheating. You can't reach in and prevent them from getting where they want to go. You have to be there. That's the focus. It's the same when you are playing against speed." Dave pointed to a few veteran defensemen in the NHL who were excellent examples of consistent good positioning. "These guys aren't fast. Most guys in the league are faster, but they don't get beat, ever, because they have excellent body position."

Checking is playing the team game. It's the embodiment of hockey tough and hockey smart. When I worked with the Nashville Predators, I spoke about the art of checking with Brent Gilchrist and Clarke Wilm, two NHL veterans who play a team game. When I asked what it took to be an effective checker in the NHL, they said, "You've got to work hard, skate hard, be physical, and stay in your opponent's face. However, it's a controlled aggression. You can't run at guys. You have to be aware of positioning and where you are on the ice. It's important to maintain good angles." When I asked what they meant by good angles, they replied, "It's angling a player where you want them to go, not where they want to go."

Matt Cooke, the Vancouver Canucks winger, says speed and determination have helped him be an effective checker and penalty killer in the NHL. Matt added that one thing he's learned over the last few years that has helped him be more effective defensively is to moderate his speed. "You can't go full speed 100 percent all the time. You have to play smart and learn when and where to turn it on."

Good checkers and good penalty killers take pride in shutting out an opponent's scoring line. The better the line, the bigger the challenge. It's not an easy role to play. A positive attitude toward the challenge makes the job easier.

If you are given the role of checker, embrace the assignment. Assume the identity; become the best checker you can be. Imagine yourself as the other player's shadow or as a tiger on the hunt. Remember what Mark Messier said: "You can create a winning mind-set by playing a solid team game. It's important that all the players believe they contribute and make a difference. Whether a guy plays 30 minutes or 5 minutes, whether he's a scorer or a checker, when everyone believes they make a difference and play like they make a difference, remarkable things can happen. I've seen it."

# CHAPTER 11

# Stoning the Opposition in Goal

No job in professional sport is more pressure and stress filled than being a goalkeeper in the NHL. A major source of this pressure is that a goalie's performance can impact a team's mindset and confidence. I asked a veteran Buffalo Sabres player what it was like playing in front of Dominik Hasek when he was in his prime. "It was inspiring. You knew that the guy could stop anything. It lifts your game. It gave me a kind of confidence, and at the same time it challenged me to hold up my end of the bargain."

In contrast, I spoke with an NHL player and longtime client following a series of games in which his team had played hard but lost, in part because it seemed that the goalie had allowed a soft goal or two each game. The impact on his confidence was obvious. "Your goal is like your home. Lately I've been getting this uncomfortable feeling like I've left home and I'm not sure if I locked the door or not."

Many goalies feel the pressure. I have worked with goalies who didn't speak on game days, goalies who vomited before games, and goalies who talked to their goalposts. One NHL goalie's wife described her husband as becoming so tense during the season that he would kick out his legs and flail his arms in his sleep, as if making imaginary saves. I'm sure that made it very difficult to be in the same bed with him! To survive—and thrive—in that high-pressure environment, a goalie, more than any other player, must master the mental game.

**Imagine a job where every time you make a mistake a red light flashes and 15,000 people stand up and cheer.**

*Jacques Plante, NHL Hall of Fame goalie*

The three things a goalie must learn to manage are his focus, his emotions, and his attitude. Of course, these are the same three qualities that any player must master, but the challenges goalies face are unique and more intense. Everyone can make a mistake, but for the goalie, the puck (and accountability) stops here!

1. **Focus** is a key element of a goalie's success. A goalie has to maintain sharp focus on the play and the puck for long time periods. He must know who is on the ice and where they are. He must fight for clear sight lines to the puck. He must also be able to tune out distractions such as being jostled or bumped in the crease, and cannot allow a soft goal to bother him. Nothing must affect his focus or judgment. Many of the focusing techniques described in chapters 2 and 3, such as using positive self-talk, having clear ABCs, being the cat, and seeing yourself making the plays, can help a goalie stay on a positive track.

2. A goalie must maintain **emotional control**. Tending goal means tending your emotions. A shift can last the full 60 minutes, during which you must maintain a razor-sharp edge. To survive and excel, you have to stay sharp and keenly focused, be on edge as the puck moves toward your end of the rink, and then be able to release unnecessary tension when the pressure subsides. A key to mastering your emotions and playing winning hockey is to work on breathing techniques—release, breathe, refocus; turning the wheel; and being a star—as described in chapter 4.

3. **Attitude** is what sustains any player in waging the hockey wars. The key attitude components for goalies are the same as for forwards and defensemen: commitment, confidence, and a positive identity—"I am" and "I can."

# ASK THE PROS

I asked several experienced NHL goalies what they thought was key to the mental game. Glen Hanlon played in the NHL for 13 seasons with the Vancouver Canucks, St. Louis Blues, New York Rangers, and Detroit Red Wings. Glen saw the game from just about every angle—as a starting goalie and a backup on both winning and losing teams. He learned to perform and excel in the day-to-day demands of the long NHL season as well as under the intense pressure of the playoffs. After retiring as a player, Glen was an assistant and goalie coach with the Canucks for seven years before becoming a head coach and winning AHL coach-of-the-year honors. Glen is now coaching in the NHL.

We worked together throughout his career, and I found Glen to be a student of the mental game. He incorporated many of the techniques I've described into his preparation and play. I asked Glen what advice he would give to a goalie on the mental game. He started by listing his ABCs:

A. Preparation

B. Position

C. Hard work

By *preparation*, Glen means physical and mental conditioning. Like Mark Messier and Tiger Williams, Glen believes physical conditioning is very important to knowing that you're fit and ready. "What some goalies don't realize is that being physically fit builds confidence. Feeling stronger and faster helps you feel better and prepared to play better. Feeling tired can make you feel slower and more vulnerable. Physical preparation is also about practicing the basics. It's using practice to work on improving your technique for stopping shots, playing two-on-ones, moving well in the net from side to side, and covering the wraparounds."

Glen continued, "Mental preparation includes mental rehearsal, actually visualizing yourself reacting well in each and every situation. It's imagining yourself performing well in the very same situations you practiced on the ice. And it's seeing and knowing that you can stop the puck in each situation. Then it's taking that knowledge into the game and doing it."

Another part of mental preparation that Glen considers vital is managing emotions. "What helped me was working with my breathing, specifically, using my breathing to stay sharp and focused under pressure and then cool and calm when the pressure is relieved."

By *position*, Glen means being square to the shooter and playing the angles correctly. "Good position has you in the right place to stop the shot. It can also force the shooter to miss by taking away the net. Hockey is a dynamic game; it's fast and ever changing. A goalie moving and reacting to the puck can get lost or out of position. A goalie must continually work in practice and in the game to adjust and improve position. Effectiveness and confidence come from knowing where you are and that you are in the right place."

The third ABC is *hard work*. Goalies frequently remind me that for most players, a shift lasts for less than a minute. In contrast, the goalie is usually on the ice for the entire game. It can be a real challenge for a goalkeeper to maintain his edge for the entire 60 minutes, which can take roughly two to three hours to play. Fatigue can affect both concentration and attitude. Being in good physical shape makes it easier to meet the intense physical demands of the game. It also helps a goalie maintain concentration, focus, and the belief that "I can."

Hard work means doing everything necessary to stay on top of the mental game. Glen said, "Whenever you notice your attention starting to slip or when you stop mentally attacking the shooter and start to feel lazy or spacey or when a negative thought comes to mind, you have to work to refocus and stay positive and sharp. That's hard work, and it's a key to consistent, successful goaltending."

As a player battling in the Stanley Cup playoffs, Glen wanted some input—something to sharpen the edge—so he gave me a call. I reminded him of the things we had worked on over the years: stay in the moment—experience one breath at a time, one shot at a time, one period at a time; and see yourself making the plays, playing the angles, stopping the shots, and being like a cat. In essence, I reminded him of the basics I've discussed throughout the book: focus on the positive (right focus), breathe (right feeling), and know that you are OK (right attitude).

Glen was playing for Detroit. At first, he split the playing time with the team's other goalie. Then, after two disappointing losses, his colleague was benched. With the Wings on the brink of elimination—down three games to one in the best-of-seven series—Glen rose to the challenge, shutting out the Leafs 3-0. Two nights later he led Detroit to a 4-2 win, then was unbeatable in the seventh and final game of the series, racking up another 3-0 shutout. Glen's play sparked his team to win the divisional championship.

The day after that first shutout against Toronto, Glen reflected on his performance: "With about 10 minutes to go in the game, I started to experience some doubt. I recall thinking, 'Something's going to happen; this is too good to last.' Then I noticed what I was thinking, so I took a breath and refocused on the positive. I thought of being like a cat, playing my angles, and being in the moment. After that, I knew I could stop anything." A moment later, he made another big save to preserve the shutout. Glen's ability to stay focused on the positive and be in the moment is the product of preparation and hard work.

Mitch Korn has been a goalie coach for two decades. During that time, he has coached some top NHL goalies, including Dominik Hasek, Mike Dunham, Tomas Vokoun, Grant Fuhr, Steve Shields, Olaf Kolzig, and Martin Biron. Mitch, like Glen, underscores the importance of preparation and hard work. He says, "Goalies have many things to consider in reacting to the puck as it comes off a stick. Is it a shot or a pass? If it is a pass, where is it going? On a shot, is the shot left, middle, or right? Is it high or low? Do I stop the shot with a pad or a glove? What save selection do I choose? Where are the sticks for a possible deflection? Where's my defense? Where do I play the rebound?"

Mitch continues, "On an 80-mile-an-hour shot from the point (60 feet from the goal), the puck is at the net in less than a second. A goalie's decision must be instantaneous. The only way this is possible is with lots of practice, quality practice—making the right read and the right save again and again, both on the ice and with visualization (mental rehearsal). With thousands of practiced repetitions, a goalie must recognize the situation and have the most effective and efficient response already mentally learned. Add to that the muscle memory that develops, and save decisions become involuntary and instantaneous. The key is lots of preparation and hard work."

Mitch reiterated that because a goalie has to compute so many things in making the correct split-second decision that leads to a save, he can only react if his mind is clear. However, if part of a goalie's consciousness is stuck on the last goal allowed, on the scorer missing a shot on the shot clock, on a negative thought, on keeping a shutout, on blaming a teammate, or on thinking about a loud fan in the stands, then he won't be there to react fully and effectively.

Mitch stressed the importance of goalies being able to control their emotions. The intense pressure that goalies face can be exhausting and distracting, but they can't allow anything to affect their concentration. They need to park goals, track the puck, and prepare for the next play. And that takes practice.

John Vanbeisbrouck, an 18-year veteran of the NHL, feels that a correct mind-set and mental preparation are the keys to consistent high-level performance. Focused hard work in practice was one part of his preparation regimen; the others were appropriate focus the day of the game and sharp focus throughout the game. John firmly believes that players must use their mental skills to put them in a place where they can excel. John's ABCs include the following:

A. Maintain good position—aggressive, square to the shooter, anticipating, and in ready position.

B. Stay focused—maintain a puck focus during the entire game, including commercial breaks; use breaks to recharge, rest, and refocus instead of going to the bench to socialize with teammates or space out.

C. Have faith and remain calm—maintain composure no matter what; don't allow anything to upset you. "If I get beat, I refocus on my strengths."

John's focus and dedication to preparation helped him excel. But not everyone has the same commitment and work ethic. "I've seen many goalies over the years who didn't make it because they didn't manage the mental game. I remember one very talented young goalie I played with years ago who didn't really know what he needed to do to prepare. It seemed to me that he was always more focused on being part of what was going on with the guys than he was on really developing his skill and focus. He used to practice hard for 10 minutes, until he thought he could stone everyone, then he'd goof off. The problem is that when your attention goes in a game and you haven't worked hard in practice to develop the mental discipline and habits to stay focused, then you're simply not able to bring it back. That's what happened to him, and it cost him."

I've observed the same thing in junior hockey, where talented young goalies who don't do the preparation and mental work lose their focus during the game, whether because of fatigue, a soft goal, a bump, or even a heckling fan, and are unable to refocus. Without preparation and mental training, many don't develop the hockey toughness needed to play to their potential.

Tony was a promising junior goalie. He was having a good game and had stopped 42 of 44 shots. His coach described to me what happened next: "There was a face-off in our end. I look over and saw Tony talking back to a fan. I yelled at him and he stopped. A moment later, the linesman dropped the puck, and they won the draw. The puck was passed back to a man at the point, who shot and scored. I couldn't believe Tony was jawing with a fan," the coach said. "He knows better than that. What was he thinking?"

I was on a road trip with the team, so the coach asked me to talk with Tony about his focus. We met the morning after the game. I acknowledged that Tony had played well and made a number of big saves. Then I asked him what had happened with the fan. "I don't know what happened," he replied. "This guy was mouthing off, and I just started talking back to him. It was foolish."

"Did he say anything particularly offensive?" I asked.

"No, it was the usual nonsense. You know, 'You're a sieve,' 'You're a bum,' that sort of stuff. But for some reason I started talking to him. I know it looks bad when you're doing something like that and then they score."

I reminded Tony of what I had told him earlier. When stuff happens, you have a choice: either you use it or it uses you. The way to use it is that, if you notice a negative thought, a distraction, or a heckler, you take a breath and send energy out to your hands, feet, and eyes. Be a star. Refocus on your ABCs: position (good angles, square to the shooter), clear focus (see it, stop it), and poise for the next shot.

Tony was especially upset because a scout from the University of Michigan had been at the game and he had wanted to make a good impression. I suggested that Tony consider the incident a learning experience. "Two years from now, you'll be playing in a college game and the crowd will be noisy and rocking. And then you'll hear some guy in the stands with a loud foghorn voice saying something outrageous about you. And you'll use it to hit the refocus button and make another big save—and smile."

I recall watching a 15-year-old goalie a few years ago. After letting in a questionable goal, her posture changed dramatically. Her shoulders slumped, and she suddenly looked like she was low on energy and confidence. After the game, I told her that demeanor is important. Regardless of the events in the game, she should always project confidence both to her teammates and to the opposition. I shared with her something John Vanbeisbrouck once said to me: "Never let anyone know what you're thinking or how you feel." That's especially true if what you're thinking isn't positive. I reminded her that she was the boss, and that to control her mental TV and play hockey tough, she needed to release, breathe, and refocus on the positive. It's always release, breathe, and refocus.

Andy Moog was an NHL netminder for 18 seasons, during which he won 372 regular-season games and three Stanley Cup championships. These days he's an NHL goalie coach who is respected for his experience and focus. "My focus was always first and foremost to stop the puck," Andy says. "I never let the players on the other team get to me. If that happened, I saw it as a win for them. And I didn't let it happen." Andy says his ABCs boil down to position or control:

A. Be in good position—good angles and net awareness, square to the shooter, moving under control.

B. Be in control—nothing distracts me.

C. See it, stop it.

Garth Snow is a warrior. He is a very competitive, extroverted player who enjoys the physical aspect of the game. It was Garth who dropped his gloves and skated the length of the ice to get at Marty McSorley after the notorious incident in which McSorley hit Garth's teammate, Donald Brashear, from behind with his stick.

Garth believes that being bumped and pushed around sharpens his edge and helps him get into the game. However, he acknowledges that he has to be careful not to get too pumped or to take the physical stuff too far. That could result in becoming distracted or overplaying the puck.

The first thing to remember about managing emotions is know yourself. The second thing is learn to breathe, release, and refocus. For a goalie who's on the ice a full 60 minutes or more, it's essential to stay focused and in control. Garth's ABCs are five keys:

A. Focus on the puck. See it, stop it.

B. Read the slot, not just the puck. Know who's where on the ice.

C. Be compact and tight. No pucks go through me.

D. Stay square to the puck. That way, partial saves and pucks that hit me don't go in.

E. Be patient. Challenge the shooter mentally, but don't commit.

An image I have suggested that goalies use to create the feeling of being both challenging and patient is that of a tiger stalking, staying patient and in the tall grass, focused, tracking, ready to pounce.

Garth uses mental rehearsal to prepare for games. Specifically, he imagines himself responding to a variety of scoring situations and reacting effectively. Some goalies like to visualize the opponent's top shooters, but Garth says he doesn't do that. "I think if I were to mentally highlight a few first-line scorers, it could lead to my underestimating some fourth-line player. You have to respect and be sharp for everyone in this league."

Dan Cloutier, the talented young goalie for the Vancouver Canucks, said this about game focus and ABCs: "During the game, I remind myself of technical things I want to focus on. For me it's things like:

A. Cover the middle of the net.

B. Keep my pad on the ice.

C. Stay square.

D. Don't let shots go through me.

E. Be aware of where the shooter is even when the play is behind the net."

Dan refers to these thoughts as "his plan" and says focusing on his plan is important and helpful, especially when things aren't going well. When I asked him for a strategy of reacting to the inevitable soft goal, he said, "You have to forget about it. The goal's in. It's past. What I say to myself is 'The next save is a big one.' Then I go back to focusing on my plan, on the technical things, and stopping the puck." Dan continued, "It's the same if I've had a bad game. Earlier in my career, I might have let it bother me, I might have thought 'I've got to change something.' Now I have more confidence. I go back to the basics, to my plan, and know I'm OK and I'll play well."

I asked both Dan Cloutier and Wade Flaherty (another experienced NHL goalie) about the impact goalie coaches have had on their games. Both agreed that a goalie coach who understands the specific challenges a goalie faces is someone a goalie can talk

Andy Moog, a veteran NHL goaltender and coach, uses his playing experiences to help the goalies he coaches stay focused and technically sound.

to. Dan commented on how experienced goalie coaches, such as Andy Moog and Ian Clarke, have helped him balance his natural competitiveness with the more technical aspects of the game. Wade Flaherty said he thinks goalie coaches can be especially helpful to a young goalie's development. Wade related that he had pretty well crystallized a goaling style before he began to work closely with a goalie coach, Jeff Reese. However, when he did begin working with Reese, the input helped him simplify his approach, be less aggressive, and improve his positioning.

I talked about goalie styles with Curtis Joseph, one of the NHL's most respected keepers. Curtis describes himself as being more externally than technically focused. He says he keeps his head in the game and maintains his focus by constantly being aware of who is on the ice and knowing the opposition's plays and tendencies. Curtis, like Mitch Korn, spoke about getting into a state of "instantaneous awareness." He also said handling the puck, being verbal, and even arguing calls with the referee help him stay alert and on edge. He's aware of the importance of maintaining control and knowing when to calm down. Along with taking a breath, something Curtis does to calm himself when he realizes he's getting a little over the top is to apologize to the referee. With a smile, he added, "It takes them by surprise."

Not all the goalies I spoke with in preparing this book had years of NHL experience. Alfie was a college all-star on an NCAA championship team and a Hobey Baker Award finalist (college player of the year). He is one of an intelligent, hard-working corps of young goalies currently playing in the minor leagues. His work ethic, determination, and preparation are impressive for a young player.

Alfie has a clear game-day routine. It begins as soon as he wakes up with an early-morning walk during which he listens to audio-tapes that enhance his confidence and emotional control. He is careful to eat well and get plenty of rest. He trains hard both on and off the ice. He uses positive self-talk to maintain a winning attitude and makes a conscious effort to be positive with teammates. He's a good team player.

Alfie is equally clear about his focus during the game. He described his ABCs as follows:

A. Be aggressive. Compete. Get out and challenge the shooter in the troughs. Know he can't beat me.

B. Be patient, poised, mentally tough. Don't commit. Play the puck, not the head fake.

C. Be compact and tight. Have good position and good angles. Be square to the shooter. Be a wall. Know the puck can't go through me.

D. Be quick. Move across quickly and in control.

Alfie uses a variety of mental skills. He works with his breathing to generate energy, relax, and stay in his optimal performance zone. He uses positive self-talk—simple thoughts such as the following:

- Get out.
- Good angles.
- Fight through the screen.
- He can't beat me.
- Know where the sticks are.

To his list, we added a few power thoughts:

- I'm a star.
- See it, stop it.

Alfie also uses positive imagery to prepare. For example, he imagines himself with good position and good technique, making all the saves from all the shooters. He said he also uses imagery to increase his confidence by shrinking the net size.

Goalies differ in many respects. Just as there are there are stand-up goalies and those who play butterfly style, there are also different personality types among goalies. Many are like Vanbeisbrouk or Moog—more controlled athletes who pride themselves on not letting anything distract them. I would label them introverted, analytical, and technique and task oriented. Others are like Billy Smith, Glen Hanlon, Patrick Roy, Garth Snow, and Curtis Joseph—more extroverted, emotional, and confrontational. They believe they get sharper by reacting to the intensity of the game around them, coming out to play the puck, and responding to crease crashers. As I mentioned earlier, the challenge for goalies who react to pressure this way is to assess whether being reactive and getting physical really sharpens their edge or, in fact, distracts them. If it's the latter, they have to let it go and refocus. Individual differences aside, most goalies who want to excel must master their ABCs. For most, that means three things we talked about at length:

A. Good position
B. Sharp focus
C. Emotional control

Goaltending is not for the mentally fragile. It's a real hockey tough challenge. In no other position in hockey is it more evident that you are only as good as your last game. Even an all-star goalie and a Stanley Cup veteran confessed to the fragility of his confidence and ego after a couple of less than spectacular games. The solution is always to go back to the basics: right focus, right feeling, and the commitment to use the lessons of today's game to make you better tomorrow.

It's clear from reviewing what some of the world's best players and coaches say about scoring, playing defense, and tending goal that there is no single right way to prepare mentally or play the game. Players are individuals. Some are analytical; others are intuitive. Some pump themselves up before a game; others prefer to relax and calm down before they play. Some players report they regularly use positive power thoughts and mental rehearsal, while others report they don't use these tools in a systematic way. If your commitment is to be the best player you can be, then you should continue to assess and adjust and develop a mental training program that strengthens your focus, emotional control, and attitude.

Hockey toughness is not something a player is born with. It's something that develops with motivation, commitment, hard work, and good training. When I discussed the use of sport psychology with Glen Hanlon, a friend and a veteran player and coach, he summarized my thinking with this remark: "I don't care how talented or experienced a player is. If he's doing some mental training and is preparing, thinking, and visualizing, it's only going to make him better."

# CHAPTER 12

# Battling Through Injury and Fatigue

Hockey is a physically aggressive, high-speed, collision sport played by physically aggressive athletes, and injuries are an inevitable part of the game. Over the years, I have counseled numerous players with a wide range of hockey injuries. Most common are injuries to the knees, shoulders, hands and wrists, groin, and neck, as well as concussions and an assortment of bruises and cuts.

The nature of my involvement with hockey injuries is threefold. First, it's to support a player's positive mental attitude about rehabilitation and getting back to playing hockey. Second, it's to show players some psychological techniques that can actually speed healing and help reduce pain. Third, it's to teach them some sport psychology techniques (similar to the ones I've been describing) that can enhance their on-ice play when they return to the game.

No one likes being injured. However, to reiterate what I said in chapter 5, when something happens, you have a choice: either you use it or it uses you. If an injured player can accept what has happened, stay positive, be mentally involved in his rehabilitation, and learn some new psychological skills, then ultimately he may use a negative situation to become a better player and a better person.

An injury in many ways is an opportunity. It's an opportunity to build problem-solving skills and mental durability. It takes both commitment and mental toughness to tolerate the extreme efforts to get back to a world-class level.

*Peter Twist, strength and conditioning coach, Vancouver Canucks*

# AN OUNCE OF PREVENTION

There's some wisdom to the old saying that an ounce of prevention is worth a pound of cure. Obviously, it's better to prevent injury than to rehab well. Here are three strategies that can help hockey players reduce injuries:

1. Be in great shape. Injuries can happen to anyone, but players in excellent shape (in terms of strength, aerobic capacity, and flexibility) are better able to avoid and take a hit.

2. Keep your head up. The best protection you have is to keep your head up, on a swivel, and with your eyes open to see what's going on. Awareness enables you to react wisely and quickly. It's difficult to play smart, tough, and safe hockey if you don't play head's up.

3. Be in control. By that I mean two things. First, control the pace of your play. Accidents often happen to people when they are out of control. Second, being in control means deciding you want to be the one who makes things happen rather than the one things happen to. Be the boss, not the victim. Take responsibility for playing aggressive, injury-free hockey.

I have noticed that when some players experience a minor injury or trauma, a more significant injury will often follow. There are several reasons why this happens. Reduced mobility caused by the injury can make a player an easier target. Many players also compensate for an injury by changing the way they move, thereby stressing other body parts, which can lead to additional injury.

Another reason that injuries often lead to further injuries has to do with a player's mind-set. After being nicked, some players start playing a defensive, "be careful" style of hockey. As I noted in chapter 1, fear causes tension and tension produces fear. Injured players who play in a tentative and tight manner sometimes get just what they are trying to avoid. Playing hurt is painful and anxiety-producing. For some players, it can lead to an unconscious escape mentality that predisposes them to further injury and gets them out of a stressful situation.

# INJURIES HAPPEN

The increasing speed and size of players, the stick work, and the body contact in hockey make injuries inevitable. A lengthy schedule with lots of travel (teams like the Vancouver Canucks, San Jose Sharks, and Anaheim Mighty Ducks travel almost 100,000 miles each season) certainly doesn't help. Given these stressors, to be consistently competitive, a player must learn to use a variety of techniques for managing stress, fatigue, injury, and pain. Actually, many of the same techniques we have been discussing for enhancing on-ice performance can be adapted to both rehabilitation and recharging between games.

Three common psychological elements in the rehabilitation of most injuries are relaxation and conscious breathing, positive imagery and self-talk, and a positive attitude. All three of these elements come into play in the hand, groin, back, and knee injury rehab examples that follow.

## Hand Injuries

As gloves become smaller and more offense oriented, skates become sharper, and stick-checking becomes more common, so too do hand injuries. A broken hand or a broken or badly cut finger can be a significant injury that makes it difficult, if not impossible, to grip the stick. Further, the stick vibrations from a slash or hard pass can aggravate the hand.

Sometimes you can heal a hand or finger injury simply by taking time off from playing (of course, a committed player continues to work out to maintain his fitness level). However, most motivated athletes find it very difficult to take time off from playing. Consequently, techniques that can accelerate the healing process and help the player stay positive and prepare for an effective return are often appreciated.

In the case of a player with a broken hand or finger, I usually begin by suggesting that he relax and tune into his breathing. We focus on the same three breathing qualities described in chapter 4: rhythm, inspiration, and direction. One difference between rehabilitation and performance enhancement is that the primary directional focus for healing is more internal (within the body) than external (what's happening on the ice). That is, instead of a player focusing on his game ABCs, as he would when he is preparing to play, in rehab he is asked to focus on directing his energy to and through his injured hand or finger.

Here is how it works. I ask the player to sit back and make himself comfortable, with his hand supported. Then he's encouraged to relax and experience a smooth, slow breathing rhythm and to focus on breathing in energy. Next I ask him to imagine energy flowing through his arm and to direct that flow into the injured hand. With practice, he is encouraged to use his imagination to go deep into the site of the injury and to send energy directly to the spot that is injured. For example, if a player can feel the spot where there is a break in his hand or finger, I ask him to relax, breathe, and send a stream of soothing, healing energy into and through the injured area and to imagine the bone fusing or knitting.

We know from research that as people relax, breathe, and imagine their hands becoming warm, they can actually raise the temperature in their hands. It's not a difficult thing to do. I ran a pain clinic for several years, and I found that after just one or two sessions, patients were able to warm their hands to reduce pain levels. (The technique is especially effective for helping people manage headaches.) The important point is that you can use your mind—specifically, your thinking, your ability to relax, and imagery—to positively affect your physiology and facilitate healing.

By using rehabilitation imagery along with standard physical training therapy and game-related mental rehearsal, a player can return from an injury sooner and be better prepared mentally to play.

*An injury is a challenge.* In addition to pain, injuries cause anxiety, frustration, and fear. Injuries hurt. They can shatter a player's confidence and plans. They can also induce feelings of separation; being out of the lineup causes most players to feel less a part of the team. The fear of being replaced in the lineup, the uncertainty of healing, plus the anxiety over how you will play on returning, make being injured a very stressful time. These anxious feelings can be moderated by a positive attitude and a constructive approach to rehabilitation, one that includes goal setting, positive self-talk, imagery, and the commitment to a good physical therapy program.

As I've said throughout the book, when challenges present themselves, it's up to you to use them rather than let them use you. If you've been injured, use it. Peter Twist, the Canucks' strength and conditioning coach, helps players battle back from injuries all season long. When I asked him about how he might advise players to "use" their injury experience, he said, "I encourage players to capitalize on this time period, both to learn some new mental training techniques and to recondition more intensely than anyone. By doing so, a player can accelerate the healing process and return in better shape than those still in the game. It is a great chance to drive up your conditioning in season and improve specific parts of your game."

Pete Demers, the veteran head trainer of the Los Angeles Kings and president of the NHL trainers' association, said a player's attitude can make a big difference in the effectiveness of his rehab. "Over a quarter of a century, I've witnessed tremendous changes in players' thinking about fitness and rehabilitation. We had one stationary bike; now we have 15, and they're all being used. Almost everyone wants to work out. Some players show up two hours before practice to work out, and most work out after practice. All the teams have impressive training facilities. There's a widespread, and growing, appreciation that being in great shape means you play better, have fewer injuries, and make more money."

He continues, "Injuries cannot be completely prevented in a physical sport like hockey, but they can be minimized with training, good equipment, and good nutrition. When injuries do happen, attitude makes a tremendous difference in how players rehab. Some players are 100 percent committed to the rehab process. They are highly motivated to get back. They see the value of working hard and have the determination and discipline to focus on their rehabilitation. Not surprisingly, these are the ones who get back sooner.

"I've seen two players with similar injuries. One takes responsibility for his rehabilitation. He's positive, focuses on getting back, works hard physically and mentally, takes care of himself, and does well. Another player with the same injury doesn't have the same positive attitude, feels sorry for himself, and expects someone else to do the work for him. Not surprisingly, he doesn't do as well. What you think affects how you train, how you heal, and how you play."

Pete offered one more piece of good advice: "Keep your shifts short, under 45 seconds. Short shifts lead to faster recovery, less fatigue, fewer injuries, and smarter hockey."

Peter Twist also acknowledges the importance of attitude in the rehab process. "A positive attitude enhances the healing process. A negative attitude diminishes the results you accrue from physical training." He suggests that players learn to harness the power of the mind to maximize results and prepare to battle physically and succeed on the ice.

## Groin Strain

Other common hockey injuries such as groin strain, twisted knees, and sore backs all respond to a similar approach to mental therapy. In each case, I usually ask the player to relax and tune into his breathing, to draw in energy and then stream it out through the body.

To get a clearer picture of the injury, I often ask players to tune into the strained or injured area and to tell me the size and shape of the discomfort. Is it the size of a dime? a quarter? a silver dollar? an orange? a grapefruit? Is it round? oval? square? rectangular? shaped like a bar or a star? A player with a strained groin may describe the area of discomfort in his groin as being shaped like a rectangle, about an inch wide and about three inches long.

Then I ask players to pick a color to describe the discomfort in that shape. A player with groin strain might choose dark red. If I ask if there is a place where the redness is most intense, the response might be, "Yes, near the top." I might then might ask the injured player to go deeper into his breathing and, on the out breath, to imagine a soothing, healing energy flowing into the center of the redness.

Next I ask the player, if he could choose between sending warmth or coolness into the injured area, which temperature he would prefer. I recall a player with a strained groin replying that he thought warmth would be more beneficial. He explained that at first, when the strain was much more painful and inflamed, he would have preferred to send coolness into the spot, but the way it felt right then, he preferred to imagine warmth flowing into the strain. Again, I usually encourage the athlete to relax, breathe, and allow the tissues in the area of redness to relax so he can send a soothing, warm, healing energy deep into that spot.

In similar cases, I usually suggest that a player spend 5 to 10 minutes, two or three times a day, streaming warmth into the soreness. I also suggest that as he does the gentle stretches prescribed by the trainer, he should remember to be conscious of his breathing and to imagine a feeling of strength and flexibility in his groin.

## Sore Lower Back

I usually recommend that a player with a sore lower back lie down on his back with his knees up. This is an ideal position to take strain off the back. I instruct the player to relax and breathe. I ask him to focus his breathing on rhythm, inspiration, and direction. The direction is internal. As before, we begin with streaming energy—the five-pointed star. Then we focus on creating a subtle, self-induced traction effect on the out breath by imagining sending energy along the spinal column. That means sending energy up through the neck to the top of the head (A) and also down the spinal column into the tailbone and then to the knees (B) (figure 12.1).

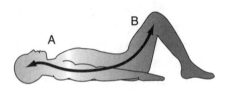

**Figure 12.1** Energy flows up to the head (A) and down to the knees (B).

For players with a predisposition to back strain, I recommend using this breathing and self-induced traction process for a minimum of 10 minutes, twice a day, throughout the hockey season. Of course, this would be performed in addition to any abdominal or core strengthening and stretching program recommended by the trainer, physical therapist, or sport physician. A player can treat both back and psyche by relaxing and breathing and doing some mental rehearsal.

## Knee Injury

For a player with a knee injury, I again begin by working with breathing—with rhythm, inspiration, and direction. With the player in a comfortable position with his leg supported, I instruct him to focus on streaming energy down through his quadriceps and through the knee to his foot. Then I ask him to relax more deeply and focus on the specific spot in his knee where he experiences the most discomfort. One player focused on the inside of his left knee. He described the spot as being about the size of a silver dollar. When asked to choose a color that described the pain, he said it was bright red.

I explained to him that when we are injured, there is often swelling and tension in the area due to tissue damage. This swelling and tension serve to protect the area from further injury. I asked him to relax and breathe, to go deep into the injured area, and to allow the tissues there to relax. Then I asked him to send a healing, soothing energy deep into the site of the injury. After a few moments of doing this, I asked him to sense what was going on in that spot and to describe the feeling. He reported that it felt as if something in the knee was twisted. I instructed him to relax and stream energy into the spot, and to imagine those tissues untwisting and strengthening.

Along with healing imagery, players are encouraged to do some positive performance imagery (slow-motion mental rehearsal) of skating well, handling the puck, head up, passing tape to tape, feeling good, and executing their game ABCs. Being mentally involved in rehab and using injury time to strengthen and develop new mental skills can help players maintain a positive attitude throughout the healing process.

## Review

As you can see, with most injuries, I advise the player to relax, breathe, and focus on the injured spot. Then I recommend that the player send a stream of soothing, healing energy into the area. I also recommend that he imagine the antidote to his perceived injury. By that I mean he should imagine untwisting what feels twisted, strengthening what has been stretched and weakened, and fusing what has been fractured.

If you feel an inflammation, you may want to cool it. If it's more of a chronic injury or something you've had for a while, you may want to send warmth into the spot. It can help to visualize coolness and warmth as colors. Blues and greens are cooling, healing colors. Soft reds and gold are warming, healing colors.

*Think heal, then imagine playing with ease.* As I said earlier, these suggestions are to accompany and supplement physical treatment and physical therapeutic exercises. The key to the psychology of rehabilitation is being positive (taking *response-ability* for affecting change), doing the appropriate physical rehab, and releasing tension *(dis-ease)* and sending a soothing, healing energy to and through the area.

As you begin to make progress, it's important to imagine yourself playing again, playing well and with confidence. If it's a leg injury, first imagine skating with ease and in slow motion and then gradually with jump and speed. If it's a wrist injury, imagine handling the puck and then shooting well and without pain. The idea is to feel yourself doing the things you do well and visualize yourself doing them first in slow motion, then at game speed.

Talking positively to yourself throughout your rehabilitation period is also important. Create and train with affirmations (see chapter 4). A few good healing affirmations are "One step at a time," "Everyday I'm getting stronger and better," and "Smoother, faster, stronger." Use the injury and the time away from the ice to improve your mental skills so that you return to the game mentally stronger and a more complete player.

# CONCUSSIONS

**I can get a knee better, I can get a shoulder better, but I can't get a head better.**
*Chris Broadhurst, head trainer, Toronto Maple Leafs, as quoted in the brochure*
*Concussion Awareness, Canadian Hockey Association (1999)*

There is both a growing awareness of and a concern over concussions in hockey. Many players downplay a blow to the head—"It's just a dinger"—and try to return to the ice as soon as possible. The problem is that a player who has had a concussion is three to four times more likely to suffer a second concussion. And if the player returns to the ice too soon following a concussion, the risk of another concussion can be even greater.

One contributing factor is that concussions can temporarily reduce on-ice awareness and slow reaction speed. Many players have said that when they are well, they have a sort of sixth sense that tells them when someone is closing in and they are about to be hit. It's as if this sixth sense provides a protective barrier around the player, enabling them to react and avoid the hit. For a while after a concussion, players report that this sensing ability is diminished or absent. They are just not as aware that someone is about to hit them, are slower to react, and are more vulnerable to a second head shot.

Players need to understand that concussions may have cumulative effects and that a second concussion is likely to be more serious than the first. Also, due to a phenomenon called *second impact syndrome*, the effects of a second head trauma occurring shortly after the first can be very serious. In part, that may be because the body's natural ability to minimize brain swelling is reduced for a time following the first concussion. As a result, the effects of a second concussion occurring soon after the first can lead to irreversible swelling, permanent damage, and even death. This is especially the case in younger athletes.

Most of the professional and junior hockey teams I've been involved with in the past few years are doing some simple psychological testing of their players to establish a mental baseline. Following a concussion, an injured player can now be retested, and the results of his postconcussion scores can be compared with his pretest scores. Significant drop-offs in performance on memory, orientation, and awareness tests indicate reduced brain function and can help determine if and when a player should return. But the test should not be the sole determinant of whether a player is ready to return.

I had a telephone call from an NHL player who had experienced a concussion with a loss of consciousness. (Note: One can have a concussion without loss of consciousness.) It had been a week since his concussion, and he told me that his memory and orientation test scores were good and the training staff said he should be ready to go back in a couple of days. When I asked him how he actually felt, he reported that he was still having headaches when he exercised and that he felt a kind of wobbliness at times. He said that even though his test results were satisfactory, his thinking wasn't as clear as before the injury. I told him that when it came to managing his recovery, he was the boss. I advised him not to return to the game until he was completely symptom-free for at least one week and tested with intense exercise (see the six-step guidelines to follow).

There's a macho code in hockey that says to suck it up, get right back on the ice, be a tough guy, and not let your teammates down. It applies to most injuries, and even more so in cases where there is no outward sign of injury. The problem is that players tend to minimize concussions. "It's nothing, I just got my bell rung. I'm not bleeding, there's no significant pain, so I'll play." And they do. However, the life consequences of a permanent brain injury are far more significant than the consequences of permanent knee damage.

Nick Kypreos, whose NHL career was shortened by multiple concussions, recalled his last concussion, which he suffered in a fight in an NHL exhibition game. "I lost my helmet and my head hit the ice. It's like a dream you can't remember. Within one hour everything started to come back into focus. I was being asked how I was feeling and if I could go back and finish the game" (Canadian Hockey Association 1999). Players should not be asked that question. They're too emotional to answer. Nick continued, "You just want everyone to forget it ever happened, to keep playing hockey. Since I was seven years old, I've been told to it shake off, dust off the cobwebs, suck it up and you'll be fine. The days of smelling salts are over. You can see a knee or shoulder injury, but you can't see a head injury, so there is always a question of how hurt is he? Only a doctor should decide when the player should return to the game."

Nick's right. Studies of professional and university athletes have shown that the majority of players who had been concussed were not accurate judges of whether or not they had experienced a concussion.

Here is a guideline for players, coaches, trainers, and parents on concussion management for recreational, amateur, elite, and professional players of all ages (Aubry et al. 2002a, 2002b, 2002c).

A concussion is a brain injury. A concussion alters the way the brain functions and can cause significant impairment. A concussion may be caused by a direct blow to the head, face, neck, or even elsewhere on the body.

Typical symptoms of concussion may include headache, dizziness, nausea, loss of balance, feeling stunned or dazed, double vision, ringing in the ears, slurred speech, or emotional and personality changes.

An athlete who displays any symptoms of concussion should seek medical attention immediately. An athlete should never return to play while symptomatic. A good slogan for coaches, trainers, or parents is, "When in doubt, sit them out."

When a player shows any signs or symptoms of concussion, the player should not be allowed to return to play in the current game or practice. The player should not be left alone; regular monitoring for deterioration is essential. The player should be medically evaluated following the injury. Return to play should follow a supervised six-step process:

1. No activity, complete rest. Once asymptomatic, proceed to step 2.
2. Light aerobic exercise such as walking or stationary cycling.
3. Sport-specific training (e.g., skating).
4. Noncontact training drills.
5. Full-contact training after medical clearance.
6. Game play.

My own personal feeling is that if the player has any ongoing symptoms such as confusion, inability to focus attention, slurred speech, emotional liability (mood swings), headache, memory deficits, or being slow to answer questions or follow instructions, he should simply not play.

I believe that following a concussion, a player should consult with a sport medicine physician and be completely symptom-free (both during and after intense physical exercise) for a minimum of a week before returning to the game.

When I discussed concussions with Pete Demers, the NHL's most senior trainer, he said, "I think psychological help is useful in assisting players who are healing from injuries. This is especially true when dealing with a concussion. Following a concussion, many players are anxious and their self-esteem is low. Some players fear they will never be right again. Frequent neurological evaluations are beneficial to find out what is going on, but one-on-one support is extremely beneficial in reassuring the athlete, helping him deal with the inevitable fear and frustration that goes with a head injury, and when appropriate, helping him return to the game."

# RECHARGING

I was talking to a first-line junior player about motivation. "How many shifts do you get a game?" I asked.

"About 20, maybe 25," he said.

"How many shifts usually decide the outcome of the game?" I asked.

"I guess two or three," he replied.

"Well, to be successful, you have to play like each shift is a game-breaker. And you have to play that way every night."

Hockey is a physically and mentally demanding game. On the ice, you are expected to give 100 percent. When you step off the ice, I believe you should have a way of recharging and reloading. I think it's advisable to have techniques that you can use to recharge as part of your pregame preparation or for postgame recovery.

One way to use imagery to recharge is to relax and breathe and imagine that you have a personal connection to an unlimited supply of energy. As you breathe, allow or imagine energy flowing to you and through you. If any part of your body feels tired or sore, imagine breathing more energy or oxygen into that part of your body. During the season, a 10- to 15-minute recharge session each day is advisable.

## Make a Script

I often make tapes for my clients. What follows is a typical relaxing–recharging script. You may want to edit this script to suit your patterns and preferences. Then make a tape of it so you have your own relax–recharge tape.

Sit or lie back. Turn off the TV or radio. Make yourself comfortable. Allow the weight of your body to be supported by whatever you are resting on. Allow the weight of your back, buttocks, and legs to feel supported.

Now focus your attention on your breathing. First, tune into your breathing rhythm. Give yourself time for each breath to come in . . . and for each breath to go out. The breath is like waves in the ocean, and the waves never rush.

Take time as you breathe to feel the incoming wave or in breath come all the way in . . . and to feel the outgoing wave or out breath go all the way out. You deserve your time.

Breathe smoothly and easily and imagine energy and oxygen flowing through your shoulders and arms and into your hands. (Repeat.)

Breathe smoothly and easily and allow energy and oxygen to flow down through your pelvis and legs and into your feet. (Repeat.)

Breathe smoothly and easily and allow energy and oxygen to flow up your spinal column and into your head. (Repeat.)

Breathe smoothly and easily and allow energy and oxygen to flow out to your hands, feet, and head, like a five-pointed star. (Repeat.)

Breathe easily and think of energy flowing to you and through you.

Remember, you have a personal connection to an unlimited supply of energy. Wherever you are, with each breath, you can tap that energy supply.

Breathe easily. Feel yourself drawing in energy and sending it out through your body.

If any part of your body feels tense, sore, or tired, allow that part of the body to release. As you breathe, imagine or allow a soothing, relaxing, recharging energy to flow into that part of your body.

Think of breathing in new, oxygen-charged energy and breathing out used, tired energy.

Remember, the breath is like waves in the ocean. Over time, the waves can wash away tension, tiredness, and fatigue. With each in breath, think of breathing in new energy. On the out breath, release tension, tiredness, and fatigue. Allow energy to flow to you and through you. Relax and breathe.

## Create a Power Place

Another thing you can do to relax and recharge is to imagine yourself in a relaxing, recharging place—a comfortable, high-energy place where you can rest, recharge, and get ready to do battle.

Many people find images from nature recharging. Some imagine being at the beach, feeling the warm sun on their body, hearing the waves, breathing in the sea air, and relaxing. Others imagine being on a mountaintop where they can see for miles, breathing the clear, fresh mountain air, and feeling powerful. Still others are at peace in the woods, beside a small lake, calm, quiet, breathing easily, resting deeply. Some choose to imagine being at home in their bedroom, lying comfortably, with no disturbances or distractions—a safe, familiar place where they can rest deeply.

You can create an imaginary space of your own. One NHL veteran player told me he loved horses. When he was at home, he would go for a ride to relax on the afternoon of a game. On the road, he would relax in his hotel room and imagine himself riding in the countryside.

The idea is that even on a plane or bus, or in a hotel room far from home, you can simply close your eyes, imagine a recharging place, slip into your breathing, and send energy streaming through your body to recharge. If you have a big game or an early flight and can't get to sleep, this technique will give you a quality relax–recharge program to tune into. Trying unsuccessfully to force yourself to sleep only produces more tension. With this technique, even if you don't sleep, you will recharge, and that awareness reduces the pressure to get to sleep, which in turn makes it easier to sleep.

Before a game, if you are feeling rested and want to do some game-related imagery, imagine playing in slow motion—skating well, feeling strong and fast, being smooth, having great hands, great wheels, and clear eyes, and making all the moves.

# LIFESTYLE

When I address groups of high-performance athletes, I usually remind them that lifestyle is an important but unappreciated factor in their continuous development and success. By lifestyle I simply mean the way we live day to day. That includes diet, exercise, rest and recreation, relationships, and attitude. As with any group, there are vast lifestyle differences among hockey players. Following are some general comments that apply to most players relative to each of the five areas.

## Diet

First, let's look at diet. When I worked for the NFL Rams, I remember cringing at some of the fast-food-heavy diets of some of the players, for instance, Cokes and doughnuts for breakfast. The players' parking lot was filled with high-priced luxury and sport cars, so I used them to draw an analogy for some of the players: "You wouldn't put that junk food in your car and expect it to perform well. Why do you put it in a high-performance energy system like your own body?"

Individual players differ markedly in terms of metabolism, experience, and preference. Some younger players feel they can eat anything (and they do) without it affecting them; more mature players tend to have developed an awareness of how the foods they eat affect performance. There are many theories and fads regarding diet, but most experts recommend a diet rich in complex carbohydrates, high in fiber, low in fat, and with a moderate amount of protein. Drinking plenty of fluids is also advised.

For pregame meals, eat something that is easy to digest. If you're like most players, you'll probably be loading on complex carbs. However, experiment intelligently and find out what works for you. Take stock of the foods you're used to eating and try to recall what has nurtured good performances in the past. One way to keep track of how your diet affects how you play is to record what you eat in a performance journal (if you keep one).

## Exercise

Most hockey players get plenty of exercise during the season, and more and more players are working out and building strength and fitness all year long. Physical training is a great way to prove the old saying that what you put in (to your training) is what you get out (in performance and power).

Work hard. You are not a machine. Whenever you can, balance activity and rest. Take a month off during the off-season and find ways to cross train. And remember what I said earlier: fitness and strength build confidence and aid concentration.

## R and R

Striking a balance between work and rest is essential. Rest is vital to good performance, and it should be quality rest. You can improve the quality of your rest by developing some relaxation or meditation techniques like those presented earlier in this chapter and in chapter 4. Getting enough sleep is also very important. Just as you schedule time for training, you need to make sure you get sufficient rest and that your sleep needs are met.

Recreation means "re-creation." The most popular "recreational" activity in North America is television, but TV is neither renewing nor recharging. Balance activity with rest, routine with spontaneity, and do things that are fun. Many distractions surround the game of hockey, especially at the higher levels. Make time to rest and recharge free of distraction and energy-draining activity. Develop a good R-and-R program.

Marty was a young player who had to play an intense, high-energy game to be effective. During his first call-up to the NHL, he got distracted by the nightlife. When he was sent down to the minors, he acknowledged that he hadn't developed any sense of balance. It was go, go, go on the ice and go, go, go partying afterward. Not surprisingly, Marty's play began to lack the jump and feistiness he needed to be effective, and he was sent down. Fortunately, Marty learned from his experience and recommitted himself to the game. Part of that meant learning how to rest and recreate in a way that helped him to be charged and ready to play hard on the ice, every shift.

## Relationships

We are social animals. The relationships you have with others are an important part of your life. Career hockey players who invest a great deal of their energy in their game usually rely on and benefit from nurturing, supportive off-ice relationships with their wives, girlfriends, parents, and friends. If you are fortunate enough to have a relationship with someone who supports you and is understanding of your needs, your moods, and your anxieties during the season, remember that the off-season is payback time, and that means it's your turn to spend time and energy nurturing and supporting them.

I remember phoning one NHL player during the off-season when he was immersed in family responsibilities. When he answered the phone, it was clear he had his hands full. He was bathing his baby daughter and trying to persuade his four-year-old son not to do something. It wasn't easy, and he knew it. He summed up his appreciation of the situation by laughing and saying, "Where's hockey practice when I need it?"

Hockey players both young and old have had careers nurtured by a significant woman in their lives—a mother, wife, or girlfriend. I remember the wife of an NHL tough guy telling me that her husband demanded that she have his pregame meal prepared for him at exactly one o'clock. If his meal was late, he would get very upset and complain loudly. Although she tried her best to accommodate him, she was a busy housewife and mother with many things to do, and occasionally, inevitably, his pregame lunch would run late. When I asked her how she handled that, she smiled and said, "Real simple; I just turned the clock in the kitchen back to twelve-thirty."

Eva, a veteran NHL wife, related that her husband frequently skipped out on household responsibilities during the season, claiming, "I've got to go to practice." She figured out what was going on when, an hour after he had gone to work, she telephoned a friend, one of the other hockey wives, and discovered that her friend's husband was still at home doing household chores and looking after the kids. Eva said, "I let him get away with it during the season, but in the off-season it's a completely different story."

Create supportive relationships that help you relax, prepare, and play the game. Appreciate what others do for you. Acknowledge their love and support. And remember, it's payback in the off-season.

## Attitude

Attitude is a matter of choice, and it's a key component of a healthy lifestyle. Choose to be positive. We talked about having a winning hockey attitude (commitment, confidence, and identity) in chapter 5. Three other elements of attitude that I would like to remind you to bring to your daily life are courage, gratitude, and love.

By courage I mean having the heart to set life goals that challenge you and the heart to work toward meeting those goals. By gratitude I mean appreciating what you have and not dwelling on what's missing. Many players know people who are sick, disabled, and far less fortunate than they are. Don't sweat the small stuff. Every day, be grateful for your health and energy and the opportunity to enjoy playing a game you love. By love I mean accepting and respecting people and opportunity in your life. Be kind and positive to those you work with and to those who support you. And do unto others what you would want them to do unto you.

# HOMEWORK

## Assignment 1: Rehab

Even if you are injury-free, find a tense, sore, or tired spot or muscle group and practice relaxing, breathing, and streaming energy to and through that area. Check out the size, shape, and color of the area. Think about sending warmth or coolness to the affected area.

# Assignment 2: Recharge

Every day for a week, spend 15 minutes practicing relaxing, breathing, streaming, feeling like a star, drawing energy to you, and letting it flow through you. Add to your recharging experience by creating the image of a high-energy power place where you can go to recharge.

# EPILOGUE

## ON KIDS AND WINNING

As I have traveled around North America speaking and consulting with teams from kids hockey to the NHL, I've noticed a disturbing trend. There is an apparent confusion of emphasis between the winning-oriented coaching of mature, competitive, elite athletes and the more development-oriented coaching of youngsters. There is a big difference in value, process, and emphasis. The problem is that some coaches and parents behave as if the youngsters' developmental, recreational game is the same as the competitive, elite game. It isn't, and shouldn't be treated as such.

As I said in the introduction, *Hockey Tough* is written for the committed, competitive, **elite** hockey player who wants to strengthen mental skills and play to the best of his ability. At the elite level, the coaching emphasis is on winning, and the hockey tough principles of positive focus, hard work, team play, emotional control, and winning attitude are all at play. Players here are seen as responseable, dedicated competitors. They play to **win**. They confront the pressure to perform, excel, and succeed. Of course, it's never win at any price. Blatant violence and intent to injure are unacceptable and have no place anywhere in the game of hockey. At the elite level, a player's satisfaction comes from playing hard and playing well, both as a team and individually, and winning.

With **youngsters,** the coaching and parental emphasis should be different. Here the focus is on nurturing an interest in the game and teaching skills and values that will make youngsters better hockey players and better people.

Bobby Orr* speaks passionately about the need for more emphasis on values in the game, especially at the youngest levels. Talking about 6 to 9 year olds, he has said, "These are our children. They

---

*Personal communication, 2000, and interview on CKNW Sport Talk, July 24, 2000.

are the future. They're impressionable. They want to learn and to have fun." He feels too many coaches and parents put winning too far in front and put the kids in positions they are not ready to handle. "There's a problem. We're turning kids away from the game. . . . We've got to let our kid go, have fun, and not overstructure them. The values we can teach them while they're having fun they can use for whatever career they choose."

I agree. To my mind, kids' hockey is about creating an environment in which children can and will learn skills, develop healthy values (competition, team work, discipline, and respect), and have **fun.** Fun is an important part of the mix at any level, but it is especially important when working with children. Youngsters who enjoy their hockey experience will return to play and learn the skills and values the game has to offer. And there are spin-offs. Research has shown that youngsters who stay in sport also stay in school.

Orr also said, "Let's teach our kids skills. They want to learn and have fun." He went on to say that if his game had been structured when he was a kid, he doubts that he would have ever developed into the player he later became.

Blaine Stoughton, a former NHL all-star who also played in Europe, echoed what Orr and many coaches have said. There is way to much of an early focus on winning in minor hockey. There is too much structure and too many games. Blaine said, "Think about it. In a game, there is only one puck and you have plenty of opportunity to work with it to develop your skills. Which situation do you think is more likely to develop skills?" It's obvious.

Frank Mahovolich agrees. When I developing hockey talent, he said, "Competition is important, however kids play too many games." Frank asked why a predominance of top scorers in the NHL were Europeans then answered himself: "It's because they have good coaching and they emphasize skill development and practice. They practice all week long. It's the same in anything from hockey to ballet; to become good you have to practice a lot more than you perform."

Pat Quinn is a master coach who has contributed to the development of many hockey tough players. I asked Pat if he thought there was too much of an early emphasis on winning. Pat's response was both a yes and a no. Yes, in that an early over-emphasis on winning can come at the expense of developing a child's abilities.

No, in that the game is about winning. Even early on it's important for children to learn to compete, to win the puck, and win the little battles.

Winning is part of the kids' game. After all, we keep score. But in kids' hockey, there should be a balance between skill development, enjoyment, and results. Harry Neale, a former NHL coach and GM, identifies love of the game as an important ingredient in a player's ultimate success in hockey. Harry believes that early coaching experience can instill it in players. Harry said, "The first five coaches you have at the developmental stages can nurture that passion. The pro coach can only reinforce it."

Again the problem is that some coaches and parents behave as if kids' hockey is the same as the competitive, elite game. It isn't and shouldn't be treated as such. When it comes to kids, it's clear—the best way to grow hockey tough players is first to grow their interest in the game, teach them skills and values, and remember first and foremost it is their game. It should be fun.

# REFERENCES

Aubry, M., Cantu, R., Dvorak, J., Graf-Baumann, T., Johnston, K., Kelly, J., Lovell, M., McCrory, P., Meeuwisse, W., and Schamasch, P. 2002a. Summary and agreement statement of the First International Conference on Concussion in Sport, Vienna 2001. Recommendations for the improvement of safety and health of athletes who may suffer concussive injuries. *Br J Sports Med* 36(1): 6-10.

Aubry, M., Cantu, R., Dvorak. J., Graf-Baumann, T., Johnston, K., Kelly, J., Lovell, M., McCrory, P., Meeuwisse, W., and Schamasch, P. 2002b. Summary and agreement statement of the First International Symposium on Concussion in Sport, Vienna 2001. *Clin J Sport Med* 12(1): 6-11.

Aubry, M., Cantu, R., Dvorak, J., Graf-Baumann, T., Johnston, K., Kelly, J., Lovell, M., McCrory, P., Meeuwisse, W., and Schamasch, P. 2002c. Summary and agreement statement of the First International Conference on Concussion in Sport, Vienna 2001. *Phys Sportsmed* 30(3): 57-63.

Canadian Hockey Association. 1999. *Concussion awareness* (brochure).

Ferguson, Howard (ed.). 1990. *The edge.* Cleveland: Getting the Edge, Co.

Gretzky, Wayne. 1996. In Glen Leiberman. Chicago: Contemporary Books.

Iacocca, Lee. 1984. *Iacocca: An autobiography.* New York: Bantam Books.

Jackson, Phil, and Delehanty, Hugh. 1995. *Sacred hoops.* New York: Hyperion.

*Legends of hockey.* 2000. Series 2, chapter 4. A Network Production.

Pascal, Bernie. 2000. *Eliminating violence in hockey.* Report commissioned by the British Columbia's minister of sport and the British Columbia Amateur Hockey Association.

Rossiter, Sean, and Carson, Paul. 1998. *Hockey in the NHL: Win with defense.* Toronto: Greystone Books.

Sather, Glen. 1996. In Glen Leiberman. Chicago: Contemporary Books.

Williams, Dave, and Lawton, James. 1984. *Tiger: A hockey story.* Vancouver: Douglas and McIntyre.

# INDEX

# ABOUT THE AUTHOR

For the past 25 years, **Dr. Saul Miller's** coaching expertise has been helping individual athletes, teams, and coaches perform at the top of their game.

Dr. Miller holds a PhD in clinical psychology and is the author of five books. He is registered as a psychologist, clinical counselor, and mental trainer. Miller has worked in more than 25 sports with Olympic and professional athletes and teams from the NFL, CFL, NBA, Major League Baseball, and PGA Tour in Canada and the United States. The NHL teams he has worked with include the Vancouver Canucks, Florida Panthers, St. Louis Blues, Nashville Predators, and the Los Angeles Kings. One of North America's most experienced sport psychologists, Miller has helped his clients set world records and win championships and gold medals.

Miller is a member of the Coaching Association of Canada and the American Psychological Association. In his free time, he enjoys exhibiting his paintings, walking, and spending time with his wife, Laara Maxwell, at their home in Vancouver, British Columbia.

Miller can be reached through his Web site at www.saulmiller.com.

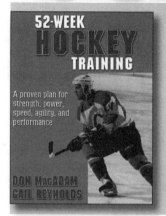
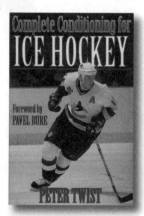